Passion Potions and Love Rituals

A Beginner's Guide to Sex Magic

Sarah Thompson

Table of Contents

INTRODUCTION 6

CHAPTER I. Understanding the Basics of Sex Magic 9

What is Sex Magic? 9

Origins and History 12

Different Cultural Practices 15

Modern Interpretations 18

Ethics and Consent 21

CHAPTER II. Understanding Energy 24

Exploring Sexual Energy 24

Harnessing the Power of Sexual Energy 26

Chakras and Sex Magic 29

The Connection Between Spirituality and Sexuality 32

CHAPTER III. Preparing for Sex Magic 36

Creating Sacred Space 36

Clearing the Mind and Body 40

Consent and Boundaries in Sex Magic 43

Selecting Ritual Tools and Materials 46

CHAPTER IV. Basic Sex Magic Techniques 50

Visualization and Manifestation 50

Breathing Exercises 53

Incorporating Sensory Stimulation 56

Partner Practices and Solo Rituals 60

CHAPTER V. Exploring Passion Potions **63**

Introduction to Aphrodisiacs 63

Recipes for Love Elixirs and Potions 65

Herbalism and Sex Magic 68

Safety and Ethical Considerations 70

CHAPTER VI. Love Rituals for Connection **74**

Setting the Mood with Rituals 74

Tantric Practices for Intimacy 76

Sacred Sexuality and Emotional Bonding 79

Healing Through Love Rituals 82

CHAPTER VII. Advanced Techniques and Rituals **86**

Working with Deities and Archetypes 86

Sacred Symbols and Sigils in Sex Magic 88

Group Rituals and Community Practices 92

Exploring Ecstatic States and Beyond 95

CHAPTER VIII. Integrating Sex Magic into Daily Life **99**

Maintaining Balance and Harmony 99

Incorporating Sex Magic into Relationships 102

Self-Care and Reflection 104

Continuing the Journey 107

CHAPTER IX. Reflection **110**

Recap of Key Concepts 110

Encouragement for Further Exploration 113

Final Thoughts on Sex Magic as a Path to Self-Discovery and Connection 116

CONCLUSION 119

INTRODUCTION

In the depths of human history, amidst the whispers of ancient civilizations and the mysteries of the occult, lies a practice that has captivated the human spirit for millennia: sex magic. Far from mere titillation or taboo, sex magic is a sacred art, a profound union of sexuality and spirituality that taps into the primordial energies of the universe to manifest desires, heal wounds, and cultivate profound connections.

Welcome to "Passion Potions and Love Rituals: A Beginner's Guide to Sex Magic." In these pages, we embark on a journey through the realms of desire and transcendence, exploring the rich tapestry of practices, rituals, and wisdom that comprise the fascinating world of sex magic. Whether you're a curious novice seeking to unlock the secrets of this ancient art or a seasoned practitioner desiring to deepen your understanding, this book offers a comprehensive roadmap for harnessing the transformative power of sex magic in your life.

But what exactly is sex magic, and why does it hold such allure and fascination? At its core, sex magic is the conscious use of sexual energy to manifest intentions, achieve spiritual enlightenment, and cultivate deep connections with ourselves, our partners, and the divine. It is a potent blend of eros and mysticism, where the physical act of love-making becomes a sacred ritual, a gateway to higher states of consciousness, and a means of communing with the divine forces that animate the cosmos.

Throughout history, sex magic has been practiced in various forms by cultures around the world, from the tantric traditions of India and Tibet to the rituals of ancient Egypt and Greece. In these ancient cultures, sex was revered as a sacred and powerful force, capable of unlocking the secrets of the universe and facilitating profound spiritual transformation. Today, the legacy of these ancient practices lives on, as modern seekers rediscover the transformative potential of sex magic in the quest for personal growth, healing, and enlightenment.

In the following chapters, we will delve deep into the heart of sex magic, exploring its origins, principles, and techniques, and offering practical guidance for incorporating it into your own life. We will unravel the mysteries of sexual energy, exploring its dynamics, role in spiritual awakening, and potential for healing and transformation. We will also delve into the rich tapestry of rituals, potions, and practices that comprise the modern practice of sex magic, from visualization techniques and breathing exercises to the creation of love elixirs and the invocation of sacred deities.

But sex magic is not merely a solitary pursuit; it is also a profoundly relational practice, offering a pathway to deeper connection and intimacy with our partners. Throughout this book, we will explore how sex magic can be used to cultivate deeper bonds of love and trust, to heal wounds and traumas, and to create more fulfilling and harmonious relationships.

However, it's essential to approach sex magic with reverence, respect, and a clear understanding of its ethical implications. Consent, boundaries, and mutual respect are crucial foundations of any sex magic practice, and throughout this book, we will emphasize the importance of these principles in creating safe and sacred spaces for exploration and growth.

Ultimately, "Passion Potions and Love Rituals" is more than just a guidebook; it is an invitation to start on a journey of self-discovery, transformation, and profound connection. Whether you're seeking to manifest your deepest desires, heal old wounds, or deepen your connection with your partner and the divine, the practices and principles of sex magic offer a powerful and transformative pathway to realizing your fullest potential as a human being.

So, dear reader, I would like to invite you to join me on this journey into the heart of sex magic, where passion meets purpose, and love becomes a gateway to the infinite. Let us embark together on a quest for truth, beauty, and transcendence, as we unlock the secrets of the universe one intimate moment at a time.

CHAPTER I

Understanding the Basics of Sex Magic

What is Sex Magic?

Sex magic is a term that often evokes a myriad of responses, ranging from curiosity to skepticism, from intrigue to discomfort. It is a practice that sits at the crossroads of sexuality and spirituality, integrating both domains' profound and potent energies to manifest desired outcomes. This section aims to demystify the concept of sex magic, exploring its historical roots, principles, practices, and contemporary applications, while navigating the ethical considerations accompanying its use.

Historically, sex magic has been practiced in various cultures around the world, with its roots stretching back to ancient civilizations. In these early societies, sexuality was often revered, not just for procreation but also as a powerful force that could be harnessed for spiritual growth and transformation. The ancient Egyptians, for instance, believed in the divine power of sexual union and its ability to connect the human with the divine. Similarly, in Eastern traditions such as Tantra, sexual energy is seen as a key to spiritual enlightenment and the realization of one's divine nature. These historical practices laid the groundwork for what would later be termed as sex magic, a more formalized approach to harnessing sexual energy for magical or manifestational purposes.

At its core, sex magic is about intention and the deliberate use of sexual energy as a potent force to aid in manifestation. This is predicated on the belief that sexual energy is known as one of the most potent energies that humans can generate, capable of influencing our reality. Practitioners of sex magic use the heightened states of consciousness and energy generated during sexual arousal or orgasm as a catalyst to project their intentions or desires into the universe, with the belief that this will aid in their manifestation. The process involves setting a clear and focused intention before engaging in sexual activity, whether solo or with a partner, and then visualizing the intention being charged with the energy generated during the sexual act.

The methods and practices of sex magic can vary widely. For some, it involves elaborate rituals, incorporating symbols, sigils (magical symbols), and specific magical correspondences such as certain times, dates, and materials that align with their intentions. For others, it may be a more simplified process focusing purely on the mental visualization of their desires during the peak moments of sexual energy. Regardless of the method, the key component is the use of sexual energy as a transformative force, directed by the power of intention.

Contemporary applications of sex magic are as varied as its historical roots. In the modern era, it has been popularized by various esoteric and occult traditions, including certain strands of Western ceremonial magic and neopaganism, where it is often integrated into broader magical practices. Beyond these more structured approaches, there is a growing movement of individuals and communities who explore sex magic as a means of personal empowerment, healing, and connection, stripped of any specific religious or magical system. This includes using sexual magic practices for self-exploration, enhancing creativity, deepening intimacy in relationships, and personal manifestation goals.

Ethical considerations are paramount when engaging in sex magic, particularly when it involves more than one person. Consent, respect, and clear communication are foundational to any sexual activity but are especially critical when the practice involves spiritual or magical dimensions. The intention behind the practice should be ethically sound, aiming not to manipulate or control others but to enhance personal growth, healing, or the manifestation of mutually agreed-upon goals. Practitioners are also encouraged to consider the broader implications of their work, ensuring that their intentions align with their highest good and do not inadvertently harm others.

Critics of sex magic often raise concerns about its potential for misuse, particularly in terms of manipulation or coercion. There is also skepticism regarding its effectiveness, with critics arguing that any results are merely coincidental or the product of psychological placebo effects. Despite these criticisms, many practitioners report profound experiences and outcomes from their practices, emphasizing the transformative power of integrating sexuality and spirituality in a conscious and focused manner.

In conclusion, sex magic is a complex and multifaceted practice that integrates the potent forces of sexuality and spirituality. Its deep and widespread roots span various cultures and epochs, and its contemporary manifestations are equally diverse. At its heart, sex magic is about the intentional use of sexual energy to manifest desired outcomes, driven by clear intentions and ethical considerations. Whether viewed through the lens of historical tradition, spiritual practice, or personal empowerment, sex magic offers a unique and powerful means of engaging with the world, opening up possibilities for transformation, healing, and growth. As with any practice that involves such potent forces, it requires responsibility, integrity, and respect, guiding principles that ensure its applications are both meaningful and ethical.

Origins and History

The origins and history of sex magic trace a complex, often hidden path through the annals of human civilization, intertwining the spiritual with the profoundly physical. This exploration into the depths of human consciousness and belief systems reveals how cultures across time and geography have sought to harness sexual energy for spiritual, healing, and magical purposes. Understanding the historical context of sex magic requires delving into ancient rituals, esoteric traditions, and the evolution of these practices into the modern era.

In ancient times, many societies held the belief that sexual energy was a potent force capable of invoking divine power, influencing fertility, and even altering realities. One of the earliest recorded instances of sex magic practices can be found in the ancient Near East, within the worship of the goddess Inanna, later known as Ishtar. Rituals dedicated to Inanna involved sacred prostitution as a form of worship, wherein the act of sexual union was seen as a bridge between the divine and the earthly, capable of ensuring fertility and prosperity for the community.

Similarly, in ancient Egypt, sexuality was deeply integrated into their cosmology and religious practices. For example, the rites of Isis and Osiris contained elements of sexual magic, with the mythological reenactment of Osiris's resurrection through Isis's magical and sexual powers. These rituals underscored the belief that sexual union could lead to regeneration and the continuation of life beyond death, a concept that permeated Egyptian culture and influenced their views on the afterlife.

The ancient Greeks and Romans also practiced forms of sex magic, though in a manner more intertwined with their pantheonic worship and mystery cults. The

Dionysian Mysteries, for example, used intoxicants and ecstatic dances to reach altered states of consciousness, where sexual acts performed during these rituals were believed to connect participants directly with the divine, breaking down the barriers between the human and the spiritual realm.

As we move towards the East, Tantric practices in Hinduism and Buddhism represent perhaps some of the most sophisticated and complex systems of sex magic. Tantra, which emerged around the middle of the first millennium CE, views the physical body as a sacred temple and sexual energy as a vital force that can be harnessed for spiritual enlightenment. Through specific rituals, meditations, and sexual practices, practitioners aim to awaken the kundalini energy at the base of the spine, guiding it through the chakras to achieve divine union and enlightenment. Tantric sex magic is about the transformation of desire into spiritual liberation, highlighting the transcendent potential of sexual energy.

The Middle Ages saw the suppression of many forms of sexual expression, including practices related to sex magic, under the rise of Christian dominance in Europe. However, certain esoteric traditions preserved and continued these practices in secrecy. The Gnostics, for example, held beliefs in the spiritual power of sexual union, which were carried forward by various mystical and heretical sects throughout the medieval period. It wasn't until the Renaissance that a renewed interest in the occult sciences, including sex magic, began to re-emerge in Western culture.

The late 19th and the early 20th centuries marked a significant revival and reformation of sex magic practices, primarily influenced by the occult revival in Europe and the United States. Figures such as Paschal Beverly Randolph, an American occultist, and later, Aleister Crowley, a British ceremonial magician, played pivotal roles in integrating sex magic into their teachings and practices. Randolph's work on sexual magic emphasized its healing and spiritual potential, while Crowley's system, known as Thelema, incorporated sex magic as a means to achieve personal and cosmic will. These figures and their contemporaries contributed to a more structured and ceremonial approach to sex magic, blending it with Western magical traditions and making it more accessible to the modern seeker.

In contemporary times, sex magic has found a place within various new age and neopagan movements, including Wicca and modern witchcraft, where it is often practiced as part of ritual magic for multiple purposes, including spiritual development, healing, and manifestation. The resurgence of interest in Tantra and other Eastern spiritual practices has also contributed to a broader understanding and application of sex magic in the West.

The history of sex magic is a testament to the enduring human fascination with the creative and transformative power of sexual energy. From ancient fertility rites to modern esoteric practices, sex magic has evolved, reflecting the changing dynamics of society and spirituality. Yet, at its core, it remains a profound way of connecting with the divine, harnessing the life force that permeates all existence, and tapping into the deep wellspring of human potential. As we continue to explore and understand the nuances of these practices, it becomes clear that sex magic is not merely a relic of the past but a living tradition that continues to evolve as well as adapt to the needs of contemporary spiritual seekers.

Different Cultural Practices

The origins and history of sex magic trace a complex, often hidden path through the annals of human civilization, intertwining the spiritual with the profoundly physical. This exploration into the depths of human consciousness and belief systems reveals how cultures across time and geography have sought to harness sexual energy for spiritual, healing, and magical purposes. Understanding the historical context of sex magic requires delving into ancient rituals, esoteric traditions, and the evolution of these practices into the modern era.

In ancient times, many societies held the belief that sexual energy was a potent force capable of invoking divine power, influencing fertility, and even altering realities. One of the earliest recorded instances of sex magic practices can be found in the ancient Near East, within the worship of the goddess Inanna, later known as Ishtar. Rituals dedicated to Inanna involved sacred prostitution as a form of worship, wherein the act of sexual union was seen as a bridge between the divine and the earthly, capable of ensuring fertility and prosperity for the community.

Similarly, in ancient Egypt, sexuality was deeply integrated into their cosmology and religious practices. For example, the rites of Isis and Osiris contained elements of sexual magic, with the mythological reenactment of Osiris's resurrection through Isis's magical and sexual powers. These rituals underscored the belief that sexual union could lead to regeneration and the continuation of life beyond death, a concept that permeated Egyptian culture and influenced their views on the afterlife.

The ancient Greeks and Romans also practiced forms of sex magic, though in a manner more intertwined with their pantheonic worship and mystery cults. The Dionysian Mysteries, for example, used intoxicants and ecstatic dances to reach altered states of consciousness, where sexual acts performed during these rituals were believed to connect participants directly with the divine, breaking down the barriers between the human and the spiritual realm.

As we move towards the East, Tantric practices in Hinduism and Buddhism represent perhaps some of the most sophisticated and complex systems of sex magic. Tantra, which emerged around the middle of the first millennium CE, views the physical body as a sacred temple and sexual energy as a vital force that can be harnessed for spiritual enlightenment. Through specific rituals, meditations, and sexual practices, practitioners aim to awaken the kundalini energy at the base of the spine, guiding it through the chakras to achieve divine union and enlightenment. Tantric sex magic is about the transformation of desire into spiritual liberation, highlighting the transcendent potential of sexual energy.

The Middle Ages saw the suppression of many forms of sexual expression, including practices related to sex magic, under the rise of Christian dominance in Europe. However, certain esoteric traditions preserved and continued these practices in secrecy. The Gnostics, for example, held beliefs in the spiritual power of sexual union, which were carried forward by various mystical and heretical sects throughout the medieval period. It wasn't until the Renaissance that a renewed interest in the occult sciences, including sex magic, began to re-emerge in Western culture.

The late 19th and the early 20th centuries marked a significant revival and reformation of sex magic practices, primarily influenced by the occult revival in Europe and the United States. Figures such as Paschal Beverly Randolph, an American occultist, and later, Aleister Crowley, a British ceremonial magician, played pivotal roles in integrating sex magic into their teachings and practices. Randolph's work on sexual magic emphasized its healing and spiritual potential, while Crowley's system, known as Thelema, incorporated sex magic as a means to achieve personal and cosmic will. These figures and their contemporaries contributed to a more structured and ceremonial approach to sex magic, blending it with Western magical traditions and making it more accessible to the modern seeker.

In contemporary times, sex magic has found a place within various new age and neopagan movements, including Wicca and modern witchcraft, where it is often practiced as part of ritual magic for multiple purposes, including spiritual development, healing, and manifestation. The resurgence of interest in Tantra and other Eastern spiritual practices has also contributed to a broader understanding and application of sex magic in the West.

The history of sex magic is a testament to the enduring human fascination with the creative and transformative power of sexual energy. From ancient fertility rites to modern esoteric practices, sex magic has evolved, reflecting the changing dynamics of society and spirituality. Yet, at its core, it remains a profound way of connecting with the divine, harnessing the life force that permeates all existence, and tapping into the deep wellspring of human potential. As we continue to explore and understand the nuances of these practices, it becomes clear that sex magic is not merely a relic of the past but a living tradition that continues to evolve as well as adapt to the needs of contemporary spiritual seekers.

Modern Interpretations

The practice of sex magic, a tradition where sexual energy is used for spiritual, magical, or healing purposes, varies significantly across different cultures around the world. Each culture brings its unique perspective, rituals, and purposes to these practices, reflecting broader beliefs about the nature of the universe, the divine, and the role of human beings within it. This section explores the rich diversity of sex magic practices across various cultural landscapes, from the ancient rites of Mesopotamia to the contemporary applications in Western esoteric traditions.

In ancient Mesopotamia, sacred sexuality was integral to worship, particularly in the cults of Ishtar and Inanna. These deities, associated with love, beauty, sex, and fertility, were venerated through rituals that included hieros gamos, or sacred marriage ceremonies. These rites involved sexual unions between the king and a high priestess, representing the god and goddess. It was believed that these acts ensured fertility and prosperity for the land and its people, linking the act of creation directly with the divine.

Turning to the East, Tantra is perhaps one of the most well-known and widespread forms of sex magic, originating in medieval India. Tantric practices view sexual energy as a potent force that can be utilized for spiritual awakening as well as enlightenment. Unlike many Western concepts of sexuality, which have often been imbued with notions of sin and guilt, Tantra sees sexuality as a sacred act that mirrors the cosmic play of creation, maintenance, and destruction. Through rituals, meditations, and specific sexual practices, practitioners aim to awaken and raise kundalini energy, achieving states of consciousness that transcend ordinary reality and lead to spiritual liberation.

In ancient Egypt, sexuality was also deeply intertwined with religious and magical practices. For instance, the mythology of Isis and Osiris contains elements of sexual magic. Isis used her magical powers, along with her sexuality, to resurrect Osiris, demonstrating the life-giving and transformative power of sexual union. The Egyptians also practiced sex magic rituals aimed at harnessing sexual energy for healing and protection and to ensure the fertility of both the land and its people.

The Western esoteric tradition, particularly within the context of ceremonial magic and occultism, has its own history of sex magic practices. In the late 19th and early 20th centuries, figures like Paschal Beverly Randolph and Aleister Crowley were instrumental in developing and popularizing sex magic in the West. Randolph emphasized the spiritual and healing aspects of sex magic, while Crowley incorporated it into his broader magical system, Thelema, as a means to achieve the "Great Work," or the realization of one's true will. These practices often involve elaborate rituals, the use of magical symbols and talismans, and the intention to bring about specific outcomes through the directed will and sexual energy.

In contemporary times, the resurgence of interest in pagan and neo-pagan traditions has brought with it a revival of sex magic practices, particularly within Wicca and modern witchcraft. Here, sex magic is often seen as a natural extension of the reverence for life and the cycles of nature, with the Great Rite—symbolic or actual sexual union—serving as a powerful ritual for invoking divine energy and manifesting change. These practices are typically rooted in a deep respect for consent and the ethical use of magical power, reflecting modern values alongside ancient traditions.

The practice of sex magic in modern Western cultures also intersects with movements for sexual liberation and healing. Many practitioners view sex magic as a path to healing sexual trauma, reclaiming agency, and celebrating sexuality as a source of power and joy. Workshops, books, and communities dedicated to the exploration of sacred sexuality often draw on a synthesis of ancient practices and contemporary psycho-spiritual insights, aiming to reconnect individuals to the transformative power of sexual energy.

Across these diverse cultural landscapes, several common themes emerge in the practice of sex magic. Firstly, there is a universal recognition of sexual energy as a potent force for creation, transformation, and connection with the divine. Secondly, the intentionality behind the act—whether for healing, spiritual enlightenment, or manifesting will—is paramount. Finally, there is an acknowledgment of the deep connection between the physical as well as the spiritual, and the ability of sexual union to bridge these realms.

In conclusion, the practice of sex magic spans a broad spectrum of cultural traditions, each with its unique rituals, beliefs, and purposes. From the ancient fertility rites of Mesopotamia to the sophisticated spiritual practices of Tantra, from the esoteric traditions of the West to the contemporary movements for sexual healing and liberation, sex magic remains a powerful means of exploring the mysteries of life, the universe, and our place within it. Through the conscious harnessing of sexual energy, practitioners across time and cultures have sought to tap into the wellspring of human potential, using this most basic and profound act of creation to touch the divine, transform their reality, and heal their deepest wounds.

Ethics and Consent

The intersection of ethics and consent in the realm of sex magic is a critical area of consideration, embodying the principles of respect, autonomy, and integrity. As a practice that combines the potent forces of sexuality and spirituality, sex magic requires a deep understanding and adherence to ethical guidelines, particularly around the issue of consent. This section delves into the ethical considerations inherent in sex magic, emphasizing the importance of consent, the implications of power dynamics, and the responsibility of practitioners to navigate these waters with care and respect.

At its core, sex magic is about the intentional use of sexual energy for spiritual, healing, or manifestational purposes. This can involve solo practices, where the individual harnesses their sexual energy towards a specific intention, or partnered practices, where sexual energy is shared and directed collaboratively. In both cases, but particularly in the latter, the principles of ethics and consent are paramount. Consent in this context goes beyond the mere agreement to engage in sexual activity; it encompasses an understanding and agreement on the spiritual intentions and outcomes of the practice, ensuring all parties are fully informed and in alignment.

Ethical practice in sex magic requires a foundation of mutual respect and trust, where all participants feel safe, valued, and heard. This is especially important given the vulnerable nature of sexual activities and the added dimension of spiritual work. Practitioners must ensure that consent is not only given freely and enthusiastically but that it is also informed and ongoing. This means all parties involved have a clear understanding of what the practice will entail and are comfortable communicating their boundaries, desires, and any changes in their consent at any point.

Power dynamics present a significant ethical consideration in sex magic. Given that sex magic can be practiced within the context of teacher-student, initiator-initiate, or even within personal relationships where one party has more experience, it is crucial to acknowledge and address the potential for power imbalances. Ethical practice involves recognizing these dynamics and taking active steps to mitigate their impact, ensuring that consent is not coerced or influenced by unequal power relationships. Practitioners in positions of authority or influence must be particularly vigilant in maintaining professional boundaries and ensuring that their interactions are based on mutual respect and consent.

Another critical aspect of ethics in sex magic is the intention behind the practice. Ethical sex magic is conducted with intentions that respect the autonomy and well-being of all involved, avoiding any aims that seek to manipulate, control, or harm others. This reflects a broader principle in many magical traditions, where manipulating others' will is considered unethical. Practitioners must examine their intentions closely, ensuring they align with principles of harmlessness and the highest good for all involved.

The role of confidentiality and privacy in sex magic cannot be overstated. Ethical practice involves respecting the privacy of all participants, ensuring that the details of the practice, including identities, intentions, and experiences, are kept confidential unless explicit consent is given to share them. This confidentiality is crucial for creating a safe space where individuals feel free to explore and express their sexuality and spirituality without fear of judgment, exposure, or retaliation.

In contemporary practice, the conversation around ethics and consent in sex magic is also influenced by broader societal discussions about sexual consent, autonomy, and rights. This has led to an increased emphasis on explicit, affirmative consent processes, the importance of ongoing communication, and the recognition of consent as a dynamic and revocable agreement. Modern practitioners of sex magic are encouraged to integrate these principles into their practice, reflecting a commitment to ethical integrity and the well-being of all participants.

Furthermore, the integration of ethics and consent in sex magic extends to the acknowledgment and honoring of individual identity and expression. This includes respecting participants' gender identities, sexual orientations, and relationship structures, ensuring that sex magic practices are inclusive, affirming, and respectful of diversity. Practitioners must be aware of and sensitive to the unique vulnerabilities and power dynamics that may arise from societal marginalization and strive to create empowering and healing practices for all involved.

In conclusion, the ethics and consent of sex magic are foundational to its practice, ensuring that it is conducted in a manner that respects the dignity, autonomy, and spirituality of all participants. By adhering to principles of informed, ongoing consent, addressing power dynamics, ensuring confidentiality, and approaching the practice with integrity and respect, practitioners can navigate the potent intersection of sexuality and spirituality ethically and responsibly. As sex magic continues to evolve within contemporary spiritual landscapes, the ongoing dialogue around ethics and consent will remain crucial, guiding practitioners towards practices that honor the sacredness of sexual energy and the transformative potential of this ancient art.

CHAPTER II

Understanding Energy

Exploring Sexual Energy

Sexual energy is an intrinsic and potent aspect of human existence, weaving through the tapestry of our lives with the power to create, transform, and heal. This section delves into the multifaceted nature of sexual energy, exploring its definitions, dimensions, and its pivotal role in personal development, relationships, and spiritual practices. By examining the perspectives of various cultures, scientific research, and psycho-spiritual frameworks, we aim to uncover the depth and breadth of sexual energy's influence on our lives.

At its core, sexual energy is the life force that propels us toward connection, creativity, and vitality. It transcends the physical act of sex, encompassing a broader spectrum of emotional, psychological, and spiritual dimensions. Ancient civilizations recognized this force, often equating it with the primal energy that creates and sustains life. In Hinduism, for instance, this energy is referred to as kundalini. Kundalini is a dormant power that is located at the base of the spine and, when awakened, may result to heightened states of consciousness and enlightenment. Similarly, Taoist traditions view sexual energy as a key component of physical and spiritual health, advocating for practices that cultivate, circulate, and harmonize this energy within the body.

The exploration of sexual energy also intersects with the field of psychology, particularly within the work of Carl Jung. Jung introduced the concept of libido as a psychic energy that drives all human behavior, not just sexual activity. From this perspective, sexual energy is a dynamic component of our psyche, influencing our motivations, desires, and creative expressions. This view opens up a broader understanding of sexual energy as a fundamental force that can be channeled into various aspects of our lives, including art, innovation, and the pursuit of knowledge.

Contemporary discussions increasingly examine sexual energy through the lens of energy medicine and holistic health practices. These perspectives consider sexual energy a vital force that can be harnessed for healing, balancing the body's energy systems, and enhancing well-being. Practices such as qigong, tantra, and certain forms of yoga focus on cultivating and managing sexual energy, teaching individuals how to tap into this force to improve health, increase vitality, and develop a deeper connection with themselves and others.

The role of sexual energy in relationships is another significant area of exploration. It is not only the foundation of sexual attraction and desire but also a vital component of intimacy and emotional connection. Sexual energy, when shared between partners respectfully and consensually, can deepen bonds, enhance communication, and foster a profound sense of unity. Many relationship experts and therapists emphasize the importance of understanding and nurturing sexual energy within partnerships, recognizing its power to sustain and rejuvenate the connection over time.

Moreover, the exploration of sexual energy is not without its challenges and shadows. Misunderstandings, repressions, and traumas related to sexual energy can lead to personal and interpersonal difficulties, affecting one's ability to express and enjoy this aspect of human experience fully. The journey towards healing and reclaiming sexual energy often involves confronting these shadows, working through past traumas, and developing a healthy, integrated understanding of one's sexuality. This process is not only healing on a personal level but also contributes to broader societal shifts toward more open, respectful, and enlightened attitudes toward sexuality.

The intersection of sexual energy and spirituality represents a convergence of the most fundamental aspects of human experience. Many spiritual traditions and modern practices view sexual energy as a gateway to divine connection, a tool for transcending the ego, and a path to higher states of consciousness. This perspective highlights the sacredness of sexual energy, encouraging its expression in ways that are aligned with spiritual growth, ethical principles, and the pursuit of deeper truth and meaning.

In conclusion, sexual energy is a complex and dynamic force that permeates every aspect of human life. From its roots in ancient spiritual traditions to its implications for modern psychology, health, relationships, and personal growth, sexual energy offers a rich field of exploration and discovery. Understanding and cultivating this energy with awareness, respect, and intention can lead to profound transformations, enhancing our experience of life, love, and the interconnectedness of all things. As we continue to explore and embrace the full spectrum of sexual energy, we open ourselves to the possibilities of healing, creativity, and spiritual evolution, tapping into one of the most powerful forces available to us as human beings.

Harnessing the Power of Sexual Energy

Sexual energy is one of the most potent and primal forces in human existence, capable of much more than the mere act of procreation. It is the wellspring of vitality, creativity, and spiritual awakening. Harnessing the power of sexual energy is a practice that spans across various cultures and spiritual traditions, each offering unique insights into its profound potential. This section explores the diverse methods and philosophies surrounding the cultivation and utilization of sexual energy, highlighting its significance in personal development, healing, and the pursuit of a more profound connection with the universal life force.

The ancient practice of Tantra, originating in Hindu and Buddhist traditions, presents one of the most comprehensive systems for understanding and working with sexual energy. Tantra teaches that sexual energy is a manifestation of the divine, capable of not only creating life but also facilitating spiritual enlightenment. By engaging in specific rituals and meditations, practitioners learn to elevate their sexual energy beyond physical gratification, transforming it into a tool for spiritual growth and union with the divine. This approach emphasizes the sacredness of the body and sexuality, challenging the dualistic view that separates the spiritual from the physical.

In parallel, Taoist sexual practices offer another rich vein of wisdom on harnessing sexual energy. The Taoists view sexual energy as a key component of one's overall health and longevity. Techniques which include Qi Gong and Tai Chi cultivate life force energy (Qi), including sexual vitality. Through practices like the Microcosmic Orbit, practitioners learn to circulate this energy throughout the body, enhancing physical health, emotional balance, and spiritual awareness. Taoist sexual alchemy also teaches methods for converting sexual energy into higher spiritual energy, thereby advancing one's spiritual development.

The Western esoteric tradition, particularly within the realms of Hermeticism and modern occult practices, also acknowledges the power of sexual energy. In these traditions, sexual energy is often equated with the creative forces of the universe, capable of influencing the material and spiritual worlds. Ceremonial magicians and practitioners of sex magic use sexual energy as a means to manifest their will, directing this potent force with intention and ritual towards achieving specific outcomes. This approach underscores the belief in the interconnectedness of all things and the ability of the human will, when combined with the primal forces of nature, to effect change in the world.

Contemporary psychology and energy medicine bring a different perspective to the conversation, focusing on the healing and transformative potential of sexual energy. From a psychological standpoint, a healthy expression of sexual energy is fundamental to overall well-being. Therapists and healers work with individuals to heal sexual traumas and repressions, aiming to release blocked or stagnant energy and promote a healthy flow of life force throughout the body. Techniques such as somatic experiencing, tantra therapy, and kundalini yoga are employed to help individuals reconnect with their sexual energy in a healing and empowering way.

Moreover, the cultivation of sexual energy is increasingly being recognized for its role in personal development and the enhancement of creativity and vitality. Artists, writers, and creatives of all kinds have tapped into their sexual energy as a source of inspiration and innovation. The practice of transmuting sexual energy into creative pursuits is a testament to its versatility and power, demonstrating that this energy, when harnessed and directed consciously, can fuel nearly any aspect of human endeavor.

Within the context of relationships, the conscious cultivation and exchange of sexual energy can deepen intimacy and connection between partners. Practices focusing on mindful sexuality, such as conscious touch, eye gazing, and synchronized breathing, can enhance the emotional and energetic bond between partners. By treating sexual exchange as a sacred and intentional act, couples can explore new depths of connection and mutual understanding, further solidifying the foundation of their relationship.

The ethical dimensions of harnessing sexual energy cannot be overstated. It requires a deep respect for oneself and others, acknowledging the responsibility that comes with wielding such a powerful force. Practitioners must approach these practices with integrity, ensuring that actions are consensual, respectful, and aligned with the highest good for all involved. This ethical framework is essential for maintaining the purity and potency of sexual energy as a tool for personal and spiritual growth.

In conclusion, harnessing the power of sexual energy is a multifaceted practice that encompasses spiritual, physical, and psychological dimensions. Whether through ancient spiritual traditions, modern therapeutic techniques, or creative and relational explorations, the conscious cultivation and utilization of sexual energy offer profound opportunities for transformation and growth. By approaching these practices with reverence, intention, and ethics, individuals can unlock the full potential of their sexual energy, experiencing greater vitality, deeper connections, and an expanded sense of spiritual awareness. As we continue to explore and understand the mysteries of sexual energy, we open ourselves to the endless possibilities it holds for healing, creation, and the evolution of consciousness.

Chakras and Sex Magic

The intricate interplay between the chakras, the energy centers within the human body, and the practice of sex magic is a topic of profound depth and significance. This relationship, rooted in ancient wisdom and spiritual traditions, offers a unique lens through which we can understand the transformational potential of sexual energy when it is consciously harnessed and directed through the chakras. This section delves into the foundational concepts of chakras, their connection to sex magic, and how this symbiotic relationship can facilitate personal and spiritual growth.

The seven fundamental energy centers that are positioned down the spine, beginning at the base of the spine and ending at the top of the head, are referred to as the chakra system. This system originates from ancient Indian spirituality. Each chakra is associated with certain aspects of our physical, emotional, and spiritual well-being. The practice of sex magic, which involves the intentional use of sexual energy for magical or manifestational purposes, can deeply interact with and influence the chakra system, leading to profound transformations within the practitioner.

At the base of the spine lies the root chakra, Muladhara, representing our connection to the physical world, survival instincts, and foundational energy. It is here that the raw, primal energy of sex magic begins, offering a powerful grounding force. The sacral chakra, Svadhisthana, located in the lower abdomen, governs sexuality, creativity, and emotional balance. It is the primary reservoir of sexual energy and, when engaged through sex magic, can unlock deep-seated creativity and a heightened sense of emotional intuition.

Moving up, the solar plexus chakra, Manipura, situated around the stomach area, symbolizes personal power, self-esteem, and the ability to enact change in the world. The practice of sex magic, by channeling sexual energy through Manipura, can empower an individual, bolstering confidence and the will to manifest desires into reality. The heart chakra, Anahata, at the center of the chest, represents love, compassion, and connection. Sex magic that focuses on this chakra can enhance one's capacity for love and deepen connections with others, harmonizing sexual energy with the vibrations of unconditional love.

The throat chakra, Vishuddha, is associated with communication, truth, and expression. Integrating sex magic with Vishuddha can facilitate open and honest communication, allowing for a more authentic expression of desires and boundaries, an essential aspect of any sexual or magical practice. The third eye chakra, Ajna, located in the forehead, governs intuition, insight, and psychic abilities. Sex magic, when directed through Ajna, can heighten intuitive abilities and open the practitioner to deeper spiritual insights.

Finally, the crown chakra, Sahasrara, at the top of the head, connects us to the divine and the universe at large. Engaging this chakra in sex magic practices can lead to profound spiritual experiences, a sense of oneness with all, and an expanded state of consciousness.

The practice of sex magic, when aligned with the chakra system, becomes a powerful tool for personal and spiritual development. By intentionally directing sexual energy through the chakras, practitioners can unlock blockages, heal emotional wounds, and facilitate growth in areas of their lives that correspond to each chakra. For instance, focusing sexual energy on the sacral chakra can enhance creativity and heal sexual traumas, while directing energy towards the heart chakra can open one to deeper love and compassion.

Moreover, the integration of chakras in sex magic emphasizes the holistic nature of sexuality, transcending its physical aspects and highlighting its spiritual and energetic dimensions. This approach fosters a deep respect and reverence for sexual energy, viewing it as a sacred force capable of catalyzing profound spiritual awakenings and transformations.

The ethical considerations in engaging with chakras and sex magic are paramount. Practitioners must approach these practices with integrity, respect, and a deep understanding of the energies they are working with.

Consent, communication, and the well-being of all participants are foundational to ensuring that sex magic is performed in a safe, respectful, and empowering manner.

Furthermore, the practice of chakras and sex magic is not without challenges. It requires dedication, self-awareness, and often guidance from experienced practitioners to navigate effectively. The journey through the chakras can surface unresolved issues and emotional baggage, necessitating a supportive environment and possibly therapeutic interventions to process and integrate these experiences healthily.

In conclusion, the convergence of chakras and sex magic offers a rich and nuanced path for exploring the depths of sexual energy and its transformative potential. By understanding and engaging with the chakra system, practitioners of sex magic can facilitate profound personal growth, healing, and spiritual evolution. This journey, grounded in ancient wisdom and adapted to modern practices, continues to reveal the boundless possibilities inherent in the conscious use of sexual energy. As we delve deeper into the mysteries of the chakras and sex magic, we open ourselves to a world of transformation, empowerment, and a deeper connection with the universal life force that animates all of existence.

The Connection Between Spirituality and Sexuality

The intricate connection between spirituality and sexuality has been a subject of contemplation, reverence, and sometimes contention throughout human history. This relationship, often viewed through the lenses of various cultural, religious, and philosophical perspectives, offers a profound understanding of the human experience. Spirituality, in its essence, seeks to explore the deeper meanings of existence, our connection to the universe, and the pursuit of ultimate truths. Sexuality, on the other hand, encompasses the range of human sexual feelings, attractions, and practices. When intertwined, these dimensions of human life offer a pathway to profound personal growth, healing, and the transcendence of the mundane. This section delves into the historical perspectives, the transformative potential, and the contemporary understanding of the connection between spirituality and sexuality.

Historically, many ancient civilizations recognized the sacredness of sexuality and its connection to the divine. In ancient India, for example, the practice of Tantra saw sexual union as a way to achieve spiritual enlightenment and a deeper connection with the divine. This tradition teaches that through conscious sexual practices, individuals can harness and elevate their energy from the physical to the spiritual realm, achieving a state of bliss and union with the cosmos. Similarly, in ancient Egypt, sexual practices were deeply integrated into their spirituality and mythology, with the belief that sexual energy was a powerful force for creation and transformation.

In the Eastern philosophies of Taoism and Shinto, sexuality and spirituality are also deeply interconnected. The Taoist idea of Yin and Yang represents the balance of feminine and masculine energies, suggesting that harmony in sexual relations can lead to harmony in life and spiritual well-being. Shinto, the indigenous spirituality of Japan, incorporates rituals and practices that celebrate life, fertility, and the sacredness of nature, often symbolizing the act of creation itself.

The connection between spirituality and sexuality is not just a feature of ancient religions or philosophies. In the mystical branches of many world religions, such as Sufism in Islam, Kabbalah in Judaism, and Gnostic Christianity, some teachings explore the spiritual dimensions of love and sexual union. These traditions often speak of the merging of souls, the dissolving of ego, and experiencing divine love through intimate connection with another.

From a psychological and transformational perspective, the integration of spirituality and sexuality can lead to profound healing and personal growth. This synthesis allows for exploring one's deepest desires, fears, and shadows, offering a pathway to wholeness and self-acceptance. Sexual energy, viewed as a powerful life force, can be channeled towards not only physical pleasure but also emotional healing and spiritual awakening. Practices such as mindful sexuality, sacred intimacy, and sexual healing therapies draw on this connection, aiming to heal sexual traumas, enhance self-awareness, and foster a deeper connection with oneself and others.

Contemporary movements and discussions around sexuality and spirituality reflect a growing recognition of their interconnectedness. There is an increasing awareness of the role that spiritual principles such as mindfulness, compassion, and unconditional love can play in enriching sexual relationships and experiences. Conversely, embracing one's sexuality with authenticity and reverence can deepen one's spiritual practice, offering insights into the nature of desire, attachment, and the pursuit of ecstasy.

The connection between spirituality and sexuality also challenges societal norms and taboos. It calls into question rigid doctrines and opens up a space for a more inclusive, compassionate understanding of sexual diversity and expression. This perspective promotes a more holistic and integrated view of human nature by acknowledging the sacredness of all forms of love and connection.

However, navigating the connection between spirituality and sexuality is not without its challenges. It requires a delicate balance, mindfulness, and often, a process of unlearning societal conditioning and prejudices. Individuals exploring this path must navigate issues of consent, ethical considerations, and the potential for misinterpretation or misuse of spiritual concepts to justify harmful behaviors.

In conclusion, the connection between spirituality and sexuality is a rich and complex terrain that offers significant opportunities for personal and collective transformation. By exploring and honoring this connection, individuals can access deeper levels of healing, joy, and unity with the divine. This journey, though personal and unique to each individual, contributes to a broader shift towards a more integrated, compassionate, and spiritually aware society. As humanity continues to evolve, recognizing and celebrating the sacred intertwining of spirituality and sexuality may hold key insights into our collective quest for meaning, fulfillment, and connection.

CHAPTER III

Preparing for Sex Magic

Creating Sacred Space

Creating a sacred space for sex magic is an intentional act that honors the profound connection between sexuality and spirituality. This practice involves curating an environment that supports the flow of energy, deepens intimacy, and facilitates the manifestation of desires through the powerful medium of sexual energy. A sacred space for sex magic is not merely a physical location but a carefully crafted ambiance that encompasses physical, emotional, and spiritual dimensions. This section explores the significance of creating such spaces, the elements involved in their preparation, and the impact they have on the practice of sex magic.

The concept of sacred space is rooted in the understanding that our surroundings can significantly influence our energy, mood, and consciousness. In many spiritual traditions, creating a sacred space is a preliminary step for ritualistic practices, designed to protect, sanctify, and elevate the energies present. Similarly, in sex magic, creating a sacred space is essential for focusing intention, nurturing a deep connection between partners (if applicable), and aligning with the universal energies that facilitate the manifestation of desired outcomes.

Creating a sacred space for sex magic begins with the physical environment. This involves choosing a location where interruptions are unlikely, and the atmosphere feels inherently peaceful. The space should be cleaned and decluttered, as physical cleanliness impacts energetic cleanliness, creating a serene and open environment. The arrangement of the space can include comfortable textiles, cushions, or mats that invite relaxation and openness.

The thoughtful use of lighting, colors, and scents further enhances the ambiance of the sacred space. Soft, warm lighting or the gentle glow of candles can create a soothing, mystical atmosphere conducive to deep states of relaxation and openness. Colors play a subtle yet potent role in influencing mood and energy; for example, deep reds and purples can invoke feelings of passion and spirituality, while soft blues and greens promote healing and calmness. Scents from incense, essential oils, or natural flowers can further elevate the sensory experience, each aroma inviting a specific energy or emotional response conducive to the practice at hand.

Incorporating symbolic items or altars can also significantly enhance the sacredness of the space. These may include crystals, which are believed to hold and amplify energy; symbols or images of deities, guides, or totems that align with the practitioner's intentions; and personal items that hold spiritual significance. The placement of these items should be intentional, creating a focal point that grounds the energy and intention of the sex magic practice.

The energetic preparation of the space is equally important. This can involve rituals such as smudging with sage, palo santo, or other herbs to clear negative energies or using sound vibrations from bells, bowls, or chanting to purify and elevate the space's vibrational frequency. Setting protective boundaries through visualization or the casting of a circle can also be employed to ensure that only energies aligned with the highest good can enter and influence the practice.

The intention behind creating a sacred space for sex magic is at the heart of the process. Before beginning, practitioners often meditate on their intentions, focusing their thoughts and energy on what they wish to manifest. This process clarifies the purpose of the ritual and aligns the practitioner's energy with their desires, making the space truly sacred.

The impact of creating and utilizing a sacred space for sex magic is profound. It allows practitioners to step out of the mundane and into a realm where the boundaries between the physical and spiritual blur, facilitating a deeper connection to the self, the divine, and the universal energies that govern existence. Within this sacred space, sexual energy can be elevated from its physical expression to a potent force for transformation, healing, and manifestation.

Moreover, the creation of a sacred space for sex magic fosters a more profound sense of respect, reverence, and sanctity for the act of sex itself. It becomes an intentional, conscious practice that honors the divine within and around us, transforming sex from a purely physical act to a powerful spiritual journey.

In contemporary practices, the concept of creating sacred spaces for sex magic resonates with the growing awareness of the interconnectedness of all aspects of our being—physical, emotional, spiritual—and the universe at large. It reflects a holistic approach to spirituality and sexuality, recognizing the inherent sacredness of sexual energy as a vital life force and a medium for profound personal and collective transformation.

In conclusion, the creation of a sacred space for sex magic is a multifaceted process that involves careful preparation of the physical environment, energetic cleansing and protection, and the intentional setting of desires and boundaries. This sacred space becomes a vessel for the transformation of sexual energy into a powerful tool for manifestation, healing, and spiritual growth. By honoring the sacredness of this practice, individuals open themselves to deeper levels of consciousness, connection, and the realization of their true potential. The creation of sacred space for sex magic is not only a practice of ancient wisdom but also a deeply relevant and transformative practice for the modern seeker.

Clearing the Mind and Body

Clearing one's mind and body in preparation for sex magic is an essential phase in the preparation process, and it is important to the effectiveness and depth of the practice. A clear, concentrated intention as well as a harmonious energy flow are both necessary components of the practice of sex magic, which is a method of manifesting wishes that mixes sexuality and spirituality. It is necessary to engage in purposeful activities in order to purify both the mind and the body in order to achieve this condition of clarity and balance. This will create an atmosphere that is suitable to the growth of the divine energy that is associated with sex magic. The significance of mental and physical preparation, the methods that are utilized for clearing, and the influence that such practices have on sex magic are all topics that are discussed in this section.

When it comes to sex magic, preparation is not merely a physical act; rather, it is a comprehensive approach that involves taking into account the mental, emotional, as well as spiritual components of existence. A step that is essential to the process of establishing a concentrated goal is clearing one's mind, which is the first step in the process. It is possible for the mind to become cluttered with the worries, fears, and diversions that are encountered on a daily basis, which can impede the flow of sexual energy and the clarity of one's desires.

Meditation, exercises that involve deep breathing, and writing are some of the activities that are utilized in order to calm the mental chatter about the situation. There is a condition of present and receptivity that can be achieved by means of the practice of meditation, which enables the observation and release of intrusive thoughts. Exercises that include deep breathing, like pranayama, are beneficial for regulating the flow of energy and soothing the nervous system, which further contributes to the establishment of mental clarity. The practice of journaling, on the other hand, provides a vehicle through which one may clarify and improve their intentions for the exercise, so ensuring that the emphasis is both clear and purposeful.

Similarly to the need of mental preparation, the purification of the body is also of equal significance. As a result of the fact that the body is the vessel through which sexual energy flows and manifests, its cleanliness and readiness are of the utmost importance. Practices like as bathing or washing with the goal of cleansing, using salts or essential oils to energetically cleanse the aura, and other similar activities can be taken as part of the physical preparation process. The body's energy flow and sensitivity can also be improved by taking dietary issues into account, such as consuming foods that are light and nourishing before engaging in the exercise. Actively participating in physical exercises, such as yoga or stretching, can assist in the release of physical tension and the alignment of the energy centers, also known as chakras, of the body, which further facilitates the flow of sexual energy in a harmonious manner.

Grounding is another key component of preparing the mind and body for sex magic, and it is something that should be practiced regularly. In order to stabilize one's energy and establish a connection with the Earth's healing vibrations, grounding activities, like walking barefoot on the earth, envisioning roots spreading from one's feet into the ground, or engaging in grounding yoga positions, are helpful. Because of this connection, not only is the flow of energy supported, but the practitioner also experiences an increase in the sensation of being centered and present, both of which are vital attributes for successful sex magic.

Both the aura and the physical environment can be cleansed through the utilization of energy clearing methods. Some examples of these practices include the usage of sage smudging, sound healing, and crystal treatment. The purpose of these practices is to create a sacred and energetically clear place for the ritual of sex magic by clearing energetic blocks and bringing the vibrational frequency of the body and the environment into harmony.

When it comes to the cleaning process, the emotional body is another essential component that must be addressed. It is possible for emotional blocks or sentiments that have not been resolved to obstruct the flow of sexual energy and cloud intention. When it comes to addressing and releasing these blocks, techniques such as the emotional freedom method (EFT), shadow work, or counseling can be extremely helpful. By confronting and healing emotional wounds, practitioners can approach sex magic with an open heart, ready to fully engage in the transformational power of their sexual energy. This allows them to be more effective in their practice.

The integration of the shadow self, which refers to the aspects of oneself that are frequently ignored or repressed, is also an essential component of the preparation process. In order to achieve a more genuine and potent expression of one's sexual and magical energy, it is possible to acknowledge and incorporate these components. Facilitating this process of integration, which ultimately results in better wholeness and alignment, can be accomplished through the use of practices such as guided visualization, journaling, and mindful reflection. The influence of cleansing the mind and body in preparation for sex magic is significant.

Because of this, it is possible to engage with the practice in a more profound and concentrated manner, which in turn increases the effectiveness of the sexual energy that is gathered and channeled toward one's goals. Through the cultivation of this condition of clarity and purity, the practitioner is able to strengthen their connection with the divine, which in turn enables them to more efficiently channel universal energies. Additionally, the process of preparation itself is transforming, as it encourages personal development, self-awareness, and healing throughout the individual. The practitioner's relationship with themselves, their partner (if they are engaged), and the spiritual forces at play is strengthened as a result, which creates an environment that is especially conducive to the growth of the practitioner's wishes.

The conclusion is that emptying the mind and body in preparation for sex magic is a vital preliminary step that enhances the efficacy, depth, and holiness of the practice. Practitioners are able to create a condition of clarity, balance, and readiness by utilizing a variety of practices that involve mental, bodily, and emotional purification. This preparation not only helps to ensure that desires are successfully manifested via the use of sex magic, but it also adds to the development of the individual and the progression of their spirituality. By approaching sex magic with a clear mind and a pure body, practitioners open themselves up to the vast possibilities of transformation and manifestation that this powerful practice, which dates back thousands of years, has to offer.

Consent and Boundaries in Sex Magic

In the realm of sex magic, a practice where sexual energy is harnessed to manifest intentions, the concepts of consent and boundaries are not only ethical imperatives but foundational principles that ensure the integrity and potency of the work. These principles are critical in navigating the deeply personal and powerful terrain of sex magic, fostering an environment of trust, respect, and mutual empowerment. This section explores the importance of consent and boundaries within sex magic, the challenges and nuances of establishing them, and the profound impact they have on the effectiveness and transformative potential of the practice.

Consent in sex magic goes beyond the basic legal definitions typically associated with sexual activity. It encompasses a comprehensive understanding and agreement between all parties involved regarding the practice's nature, scope, and intentions. True consent is informed, enthusiastic, and revocable at any time, reflecting an ongoing conversation rather than a one-time agreement. This level of consent ensures that all participants are fully aware of and aligned with the ritual's purpose, methods, and potential outcomes, thereby creating a container of trust and safety essential for the vulnerability required in sex magic.

The establishment of boundaries is equally critical in sex magic. Boundaries delineate each participant's emotional, physical, and energetic limits, offering clarity and protection for all involved. These boundaries might include specific practices that are or are not welcome, using safe words, the extent of physical touch, and sharing personal energy. Clear boundaries allow participants to engage fully and openly, secure in the knowledge that their limits are understood and respected. This security is paramount in sex magic, where the depth of emotional and energetic exchange can be profound.

The challenges of establishing consent and boundaries in sex magic lie in the deeply personal and societal conditioning around sexuality and power. Discussing desires, limits, and intentions around sex and magic requires a level of communication and vulnerability that many may find challenging. Overcoming these challenges involves cultivating an environment of openness and non-judgment, where all participants feel valued and heard. It also requires education and awareness around the dynamics of consent and the importance of boundaries, ensuring that participants have the knowledge and language to express their needs and desires clearly.

The nuances of consent and boundaries in sex magic also involve the consideration of the energetic and spiritual dimensions of the practice. Consent must encompass not only the physical aspects of the ritual but also the sharing and exchange of energy. Participants must be aware of and agree to how their energy will be used and exchanged, including any potential energetic connections that may be formed. Boundaries may also need to encompass spiritual beliefs and practices, ensuring that all aspects of the ritual are in alignment with the participants' spiritual values and comfort levels.

The impact of consent and boundaries on the effectiveness of sex magic cannot be overstated. A practice rooted in mutual respect, trust, and clear intention will more likely create a powerful and focused channel for manifesting desires. Consent and boundaries create a sacred container for the ritual, enhancing the potency of the sexual energy raised and directed. Moreover, the process of establishing consent and boundaries is itself transformative, deepening the connection between participants and fostering a sense of personal agency and empowerment.

Furthermore, the ethical practice of sex magic, grounded in consent and boundaries, contributes to the broader healing of societal attitudes towards sexuality. By modeling respectful, consensual, and boundary-aware practices, sex magic practitioners can challenge and transform the dynamics of power, control, and exploitation that have historically marred sexual interactions. This shift benefits the individuals directly involved and contributes to the collective healing and evolution of societal attitudes towards sex and spirituality.

In conclusion, consent and boundaries are foundational to the practice of sex magic, ensuring that it is conducted with integrity, respect, and mutual empowerment. These principles are critical in navigating the complex interplay of sexual and magical energies, fostering an environment where transformation, manifestation, and personal growth can flourish. By prioritizing consent and boundaries, practitioners of sex magic can create powerful, ethical, and transformative experiences that honor the sacredness of their intentions and the dignity of all involved. As we continue to explore as well as deepen our understanding of sex magic, the commitment to consent and boundaries remains a guiding light, ensuring the practice remains a force for positive change, healing, and empowerment.

Selecting Ritual Tools and Materials

In the practice of sex magic, the selection of ritual equipment and materials is a very personal and significant procedure that reflects the practitioner(s)' intents, beliefs, and wants. It is essential to do this preparation in order to establish a sacred place and to facilitate the flow of energy that is required for the manifestation of the outcomes that are sought. A wide range of factors, including cultural customs, individual preferences, and the particular objectives of the ritual, can have a significant effect on the selection of suitable instruments and materials. This section dives into the factors that were taken into consideration while picking these aspects, as well as their symbolic and energetic meaning, and then examines how these elements add to the effectiveness and profundity of sex magic practices.

When it comes to sex magic, the purpose to channel sexual energy toward achieving particular goals is at the core of the practice. The meticulous selection of ritual tools and materials, each of which is chosen for its capacity to resonate with and amplify the desired outcomes, is a reflection of the intentionality that is present throughout the ceremonies. There are many other types of instruments that are commonly used, such as candles, crystals, perfumes, and symbols or talismans. The process of selecting requires not only an awareness of the symbolic meanings and energies of these artifacts, but also a profound reflection into what is in alignment with the practitioner's individual spiritual path and aspirations.

Considering that candles have the power to symbolize and evoke the element of fire, which is associated with passion, change, and cleansing, they are an important component in a wide variety of ritual practices, including sex magic. The color of the candle can be used to further personalize the ritual to certain purposes. For example, color red is associated with love and passion, color black is associated with protection or release, and color green is associated with abundance and fertility. During the ritual, the act of lighting a candle serves to set the stage, signifying the move from the mundane to the holy, and bringing the practitioners' intentions into focus.

When selecting crystals and stones, it is important to take into consideration their distinct vibrational qualities as well as their capacity to store, magnify, and move energy. As an illustration, rose quartz is commonly associated with love and the opening of the heart, carnelian with sexual vitality and creativity, and amethyst with spiritual protection and cleansing. Increasing the energetic milieu and providing support for the process of manifestation can be accomplished by utilizing these crystals in body layouts or by placing them within the ritual space.

It is common practice to make use of anointing oils, whether they be essential oils or specially formulated magical oils, due to the fragrant qualities they possess and their capacity to call forth particular energies or deities. Increasing sensuality and appeal can be accomplished through the use of fragrances such as jasmine, ylang-ylang, and vanilla. On the other hand, frankincense and myrrh can be utilized for purification and spiritual connection. A potent ceremonial act of preparation, consecration, and intention-setting can be accomplished by the act of anointing oneself or a partner of one's choosing.

When selecting symbols and talismans, it is important to consider how well they may reflect and embody particular energies or objectives. These may be sigils that were crafted specifically for the ritual, symbols of deities that are related with sexuality and fertility, or personal artifacts that have a large emotional or magical charge because of their significance. These elements operate as focus points for the practitioners' intents, assisting in the visualization of the intended consequences and providing a foundation for their actualization.

Additionally, the utilization of natural components, such as water, flowers, or herbs, can play a vital role in the rituals that are associated with sex magic. For example, water can be utilized for the purpose of purification and cleansing, either in the form of baths prior to the ritual or as a component of the ritual itself. There are flowers that can represent love and beauty, such as roses, and herbs that are recognized for their aphrodisiac powers, such as damiana, which enhance the sensuous and energy potency of the practice.

One further thing to think about when getting ready for sex magic is whether or not you will be practicing skyclad (naked) or whether you will choose to wear ritual clothing. Whether it be specific garments, jewels, or adornments, ritual attire can be selected for their symbolic value or their capacity to make the practitioner feel empowered and attuned to their aims. This can be taken into consideration while selecting ritual attire. On the other hand, practicing skyclad might be interpreted as a metaphor of letting go of society restraints and embracing one's authentic, primordial nature.

In order to select the ideal tools and materials for sex magic, one must engage in a process that requires mindfulness, intuition, and a profound connection to the purposes of the ritual. These artifacts are not only props; rather, they are imbued with the energy and importance that the practitioners attribute to them. As a result, they serve as conduits for the realization of desires.

When it comes to the practice of sex magic, these instruments and materials have a significant impact on the process. Additionally, they serve the purpose of generating a miniature version of the intended outcome, which is a physical and energetic manifestation of the practitioners' goals. Practitioners are able to more effectively direct the powerful energies that are generated via sexual union toward their manifestation goals if they engage with these aspects while in a state of heightened awareness and focused will.

In conclusion, the choice of ritual equipment and materials for sex magic is an essential component of the practice, as it reflects the level of intention and the spiritual path of the practitioner (or practitioners). At the same time as they help to facilitate the flow of energy and signify the outcomes that are wanted from the practice, these elements serve to enhance the holiness of the ritual. Practitioners can establish a powerful and effective framework for harnessing sexual energy towards profound transformation and manifestation by selecting tools and materials that connect on a personal and symbolic level. This allows practitioners to create a pathway that leads to manifestation.

CHAPTER IV

Basic Sex Magic Techniques

Visualization and Manifestation

Sex magic is a method that bridges the gap between one's intentions and the actuality of their actions via the use of core skills such as visualization and manifestation. These techniques are utilized in this age-old practice, which combines the tremendous energies of sexuality with the purposeful focus of magical intent. The goal of this practice is to transform and actualize desires in both the physical and spiritual realms. The purpose of this section is to investigate the complexities of visualization and manifestation in the context of sex magic. It will discuss the significance of these techniques, the process that is involved, and the tremendous impact that these techniques may have on the practitioner's power to shape their personal reality.

In the practice of sex magic, visualization refers to the process of re-creating in one's mind an image that is vivid and full of sensory details of the desired outcome. The technique is one that makes use of the power of imagination in order to concentrate and channel energy in the direction of a particular goal. The practitioner's will and energy are directed toward a specific goal through the use of visualization, which serves as the blueprint for the manifestation process. This technique is profoundly connected with the arousal and harnessing of sexual energy, which is regarded to be one of the most powerful powers that may be utilized for magical work. In the framework of sex magic, this practice is performed a great deal. During sexual arousal or at the point of climax, the act of envisioning the intended outcome intensifies the energy directed towards the intent, imbuing it with a profound emotional and energetic charge. This is something that must be done in order to achieve the desired outcome.

The clarity of intent is the first step in the process of visualization. This is a vital phase that determines the emphasis of the magical activity that they are performing. Because of this clarity, the practitioner is able to construct a detailed and immersive picture, which not only engages the visual senses but also incorporates noises, aromas, textures, and feelings that are related with the outcome that is wanted. If the image is more vivid and interesting, then the energetic impression that it leaves on the practitioner's mind and, by extension, on the fabric of reality will be more powerful.

The process by which these goals that have been envisioned are turned into real or tangible form is referred to as manifestation. Manifestation corresponds to the concept of visualization. Not only does it require the projection of energy towards a desired objective, but it also involves the practitioner aligning their thoughts, beliefs, and actions with their intent when they are doing the technique. In the practice of sex magic, the process of manifestation makes use of the peak of sexual energy, which typically occurs during the orgasmic experience, as a potent force to launch the envisioned intent into the universe, where it can then materialize in the practitioner's own life. A potent point of creation, when purpose can be'seeded' in the cosmos, is considered to be this moment of heightened energy and release on the planet.

Within the realm of sex magic, the processes of visualization and manifestation are not passive but rather involve active and constant interaction on the part of the practitioner. In order to properly imagine and bring about the manifestation of their objectives, practitioners need to build a profound awareness of their individual energy, emotions, and the symbolic language of their subconscious. In order to accomplish this, one must engage in consistent practice, meditation, and introspection, and they must also maintain an openness to receiving and acknowledging manifestations as they arise in their life.

Practitioners of sex magic have the ability to directly influence their own reality through the use of visualization and manifestation, which have a tremendous impact on the practice. Practitioners are able to make changes, attract opportunities, and create outcomes that are in alignment with their deepest wishes when they direct their sexual energy, which is a primitive and creative power, toward a projected goal. Not only does this practice provide people the ability to become co-creators of their own reality, but it also helps them get a deeper awareness of the interconnectedness of energy, intention, and the tangible universe.

In addition, the practice of sex magic, which includes the use of visualization and manifestation, places an emphasis on the transformational power of sexual energy. This energy has the capacity to accelerate significant personal and spiritual growth, healing, and the attainment of one's potential when it is directed with intent. It encourages a reevaluation of sexuality, not only as a physical act but also as a sacred and magical practice that has the potential to influence the very fabric of reality.

When it comes to sex magic, however, the practice of visualization and manifestation requires a person to have a profound sense of duty and to take ethical considerations into account. The conscious production of reality through the use of magical methods necessitates an understanding of the repercussions of one's goals, both for oneself and for other people. Practitioners are strongly encouraged to approach these techniques with a spirit of harmlessness, making certain that their intentions are directed toward beneficial outcomes that contribute to their own progress as well as the highest good of all those involved.

In conclusion, the techniques of visualization and manifestation are vital in the practice of sex magic. These techniques provide practitioners with a strong means of bringing their desires into reality. One can engage in a very personal type of magic that enables them to create their lives in accordance with their deepest goals and intentions. This can be accomplished by concentrating on the use of one's imagination and by directing sexual energy in a deliberate manner. The continuing potential of sexuality and imagination as instruments for personal and spiritual transformation is revealed by these practices as they continue to be investigated and refined within contemporary contexts.

Breathing Exercises

When it comes to the practice of sex magic, breathing exercises are essential methods that serve as basic tools that bridge the gap between the realms of the physical and the metaphysical. In order to facilitate the deeper connection and concentrated attention that are necessary for effective magical work, these techniques make use of the innate ability of the breath to regulate, direct, and magnify energy. This section goes into the relevance of breathing exercises in sex magic, examining their significance, the numerous methods that can be used, and the significant impact that these practices have on increasing the practitioner's ability to harness sexual energy for manifestation.

There is no possible way to emphasize the importance of breathing exercises in the practice of sex magic. As a vital life force, breath carries both physical and energetic properties that are necessary for the activation and modulation of sexual energy. These properties are crucial for the process. Breathing is considered to be a vital technique for grounding oneself, achieving a state of consciousness that is altered, and experiencing altered states of consciousness in many different spiritual traditions since it is perceived as a direct link between the physical body and the spiritual realm. When it comes to sex magic, breathing exercises are utilized to raise and manage sexual energy, directing it with intention toward the manifestation of desires. This is done in order to achieve the desired results.

There is a vast variety of breathing exercises that are performed in sex magic, and each one is designed to accomplish a certain goal. Deep, rhythmic breathing is one of the fundamental techniques that can be utilized. This type of breathing serves to relax the mind and ground the body, thereby preparing the practitioner for the focused work that is to come. Furthermore, this particular mode of breathing can be of assistance in the process of cultivating presence, which is a crucial state for efficient magical practice. Presence enables the practitioner to fully engage with their intentions and the energies that are at play.

The breath of fire is another technique that is widely used. It is a breathing exercise that involves rapid diaphragmatic breathing and is designed to accelerate the flow of energy throughout the body. This specific exercise is very useful in the practice of sex magic because it helps to awaken and energize the sacral chakra, which is the energy center that is related with sexuality and creativity. Through the activation of this chakra, practitioners are able to more easily access and harness their sexual energy for the sake of magic.

Another advanced breathing practice is called the microcosmic orbit, and it involves envisioning the breath going down the paths of the body's energy meridians instead of moving through the body itself. A circular flow of energy is created when practitioners direct their breath and sexual energy from the base of the spine to the top of the head and then back down again. This creates a flow of energy that is circular. This technique not only enhances and refines sexual energy, but it also distributes it throughout the body, which not only improves general vitality but also makes it easier to integrate spiritual and physical energies in a more profound way.

Breathing exercises in sex magic include kumbhaka, also known as breath retention, which adds another layer to the practice. The practitioners are able to build up energy within the body by holding their breath at specific spots. This creates a powerful force that may then be channeled toward the visualization and realization of their wishes. When used in conjunction with sexual climax or desire, this technique has the potential to dramatically enhance the practitioner's ability to concentrate and concentrate on their magical job.

When it comes to the activity of sex magic, breathing exercises have a significant impact on the practice. Practitioners are able to acquire heightened states of consciousness and sensitivity through the intentional control and manipulation of their breath, which is crucial for the proper channeling of sexual energy. These techniques make it possible for couples to develop a more profound connection with one another (when they are done in an environment that involves partners), increase the intensity and focus of orgasms, and provide the practitioner the ability to more accurately direct their energy toward creating the outcomes they want.

As an additional benefit, breathing exercises assist to the practitioner's overall well-being by facilitating relaxation, lowering stress levels, and enhancing mental clarity. Not only are these advantages beneficial to the practice of sex magic that is efficient, but they also contribute to a more harmonic and balanced approach to life. This practice emphasizes the interdependence of the body, mind, and spirit in the search of transformation and manifestation, and the incorporation of breathwork into sex magic rituals highlights the holistic aspect of this practice.

In addition, breathing exercises provide a physical and immediate technique for engaging with and manipulating energy, making it one of the most accessible entrance points for individuals who are new to the practice of sex magic. As practitioners improve their abilities and sensitivities, these techniques can be modified and built upon, so offering a toolkit that is both diverse and powerful for magical activity.

In conclusion, breathing exercises are key practices that are utilized in the practice of sex magic. These exercises serve as essential tools for the regulation, refinement, and direction of sexual energy. A practitioner's magical practice can be deepened, their capacity for manifestation can be enhanced, and a deeper alignment between their wishes and their reality can be fostered through the application of breathwork in a purposeful and thoughtful manner. Breathing exercises, which serve as both a preparatory and an integrative practice, highlight the fundamental link that exists between the physical and the spiritual realms. They also provide avenues to personal development and the realization of one's magical aspirations.

Incorporating Sensory Stimulation

Incorporating sensory stimulation into sex magic practices is a fundamental technique that leverages the body's sensory experiences to deepen the connection between practitioners, intensify the focus on intention, and enhance the flow of sexual energy. This section explores the role of sensory stimulation in sex magic, detailing its significance, the methods by which it can be applied, and its profound impact on the practice.

Sensory stimulation in the context of sex magic refers to the deliberate use of the five senses—sight, sound, taste, smell, and touch—to elevate the practitioner's awareness and energy. This approach recognizes the body as a sacred vessel through which spiritual experiences can be accessed and harnessed for magical work. By engaging the senses, practitioners can create a more immersive and potent ritual space, conducive to manifesting their desires.

The significance of sensory stimulation lies in its ability to anchor the practitioner in the present moment, heightening awareness and receptivity to energy flows. Each sense contributes to creating a fully embodied experience, which is essential for grounding the practitioner's intentions in the physical realm. This heightened state of awareness is particularly conducive to sex magic, where the alignment of mind, body, and spirit is paramount.

One method of incorporating sensory stimulation is through the visual channel. The use of colors, symbols, and imagery can significantly impact the mood as well as energy of the ritual space. For instance, the color red may be used to invoke passion and desire, while symbols associated with specific deities or intentions can serve as focal points for concentration. The visual arrangement of the ritual space, including the use of candles, altars, or ritual attire, can also play a critical factor in engaging the visual sense, enhancing the sacredness and focus of the practice.

Sound is another powerful sensory avenue. Music, chanting, or toning can create an auditory backdrop that resonates with the practitioner's intentions. Sound vibrations can raise energy, clear the space, and harmonize the participants' frequencies, facilitating a deeper connection to the magical work at hand.

Taste and smell, closely linked, involve the use of specific foods, drinks, or scents to evoke particular energies or states of consciousness. Aphrodisiacs, for example, can be used to stimulate desire and sexual energy, while the burning of incense or the application of essential oils can purify the space and align the practitioner with their intentions. These scents and flavors create a multi-layered sensory experience that enriches the ritual and deepens the emotional and energetic engagement.

Touch, perhaps the most direct form of sensory stimulation in sex magic, involves the conscious use of physical contact to raise and direct energy. This can include the self-touch, touch between partners, or using objects like feathers, fabrics, or ritual tools to evoke sensations. Touch engages the body fully, awakening the energetic pathways and enhancing the flow of sexual energy toward the practitioner's desired outcome.

Incorporating sensory stimulation into sex magic practices has a profound impact. By engaging the senses, practitioners can create an intensely personal and energetic ritual environment, facilitating a deeper immersion in the magical work. This multisensory approach amplifies the energy raised during the practice and aids in the visualization and manifestation of intentions, making the desired outcomes more tangible and accessible.

Furthermore, sensory stimulation enriches the sex magic experience, making it more enjoyable and meaningful. It allows practitioners to explore and celebrate their sexuality in a context that honors its sacredness and power. This exploration can lead to greater self-awareness, personal growth, and spiritual development, underscoring the transformative potential of sex magic.

Incorporating sensory stimulation fosters a deeper connection between partners when practiced in a partnered context. It encourages communication, mutual respect, and understanding, strengthening the bond and aligning the participants' energies and intentions. This alignment is crucial for the effective practice of sex magic, as it ensures that all involved are working harmoniously toward a common goal.

In conclusion, the incorporation of sensory stimulation into sex magic practices is a fundamental technique that enhances the efficacy, depth, and richness of the practice. By engaging the senses, practitioners can create a fully embodied and energetically potent ritual space, conducive to manifesting their deepest desires. This approach not only leverages the transformative power of sexual energy but also celebrates the sacredness of the body and the sensory pathways through which spiritual experiences can be accessed and expressed. As practitioners continue to explore and integrate sensory stimulation into their sex magic work, they unlock new dimensions of power, connection, and manifestation.

Partner Practices and Solo Rituals

Sex magic, an ancient and profound practice, harnesses sexual energy for the purpose of manifesting intentions, personal transformation, and spiritual growth. This practice can be adapted to partnered and solo rituals, offering unique pathways to harness and direct this potent energy. This section explores the nuances of partner practices and solo rituals within sex magic, emphasizing their significance, methodologies, and the distinctive benefits they offer to practitioners.

Partner practices in sex magic involve two or more individuals engaging in ritualistic sexual or sexually charged activities with the intent of manifesting specific outcomes or exploring deeper spiritual connections. These practices are built on the foundations of trust, consent, and clear communication, where all participants share a mutual understanding and alignment of intentions. The collaborative nature of partner practices amplifies the energy generated, creating a powerful synergy that can propel intentions into reality.

In partner practices, the act of sexual union or shared sexual energy work becomes a sacred ritual, a direct expression of the magic at play. Participants may begin with setting a shared intention, often through verbal affirmation or symbolic acts that signify the purpose of their ritual. This is followed by engaging in breathing exercises, meditation, or sensory stimulation to raise energy and deepen the connection between partners. The sexual act itself, whether physical intercourse or energetic exchange, is approached with reverence and focus, channeling the heightened sexual energy toward the agreed-upon intention.

The dynamic interplay of masculine as well as feminine energies, or the energetic counterparts in non-binary terms, is central to partnered sex magic. This balance and exchange create a potent vortex for manifestation, rooted in the ancient principle of polarity and the creative potential it embodies. The physical or energetic climax serves as a powerful point of release, where intentions are projected into the universe with the amplified force of the combined energies.

Solo rituals in sex magic, on the other hand, offer a deeply personal space for practitioners to explore and direct their sexual energy independently. Solo practices emphasize self-discovery, personal empowerment, and cultivating an intimate relationship with one's own spiritual and energetic body. In these rituals, the practitioner is both the giver and the receiver of the energy, exploring the full spectrum of their sexual and magical potential.

Solo sex magic rituals might involve similar preparatory steps as partner practices, such as setting an intention, meditative focus, and sensory stimulation. However, the emphasis is on internal exploration and the mastery of one's own energy. Techniques such as visualization, breathwork, and the conscious directing of sexual arousal toward the intention are key components. The moment of climax, in this context, is an intensely personal point of power release, where the practitioner visualizes their intention manifesting with the peak of their sexual energy.

Both partnered and solo sex magic practices offer unique benefits. Partnered rituals can enhance intimacy, trust, and connection spiritually and emotionally. They provide a shared experience of the magical and transformative power of sexual energy, deepening relationships and opening new avenues of communication and mutual understanding. The collaborative energy work involved can also lead to more potent manifestations, given the amplified energy generated by multiple practitioners.

Solo rituals, in contrast, foster a deep sense of autonomy and self-connection. They empower practitioners to take full control of their sexual and magical journey, exploring their desires, boundaries, and the depths of their spiritual and energetic capacities. Solo sex magic can be a powerful tool for self-healing, personal transformation, and the realization of personal intentions, providing a space for practitioners to connect deeply with their inner selves and the universe.

Challenges in both partnered and solo sex magic practices include navigating personal and shared boundaries, overcoming societal taboos surrounding sexuality, and the consistent cultivation of a sacred and focused approach to the practice. The effectiveness of sex magic, in any form, relies heavily on the clarity of intention, the ability to remain present and focused during the ritual, and the understanding and respectful use of sexual energy as a sacred force.

In conclusion, partner practices and solo rituals in sex magic offer distinct but equally powerful avenues for harnessing sexual energy towards magical and spiritual ends. Whether through the shared synergy of partnered work or the intimate exploration of solo rituals, practitioners can tap into the deep wellspring of creative and transformative energy that sexuality offers. By approaching these practices with reverence, intention, and an open heart, individuals can explore the depths of their being, deepen their connections with others, and manifest their deepest desires into reality. The path of sex magic, in all its forms, invites a journey of profound discovery, empowerment, and spiritual evolution.

CHAPTER V

Exploring Passion Potions

Introduction to Aphrodisiacs

Aphrodisiacs, substances that are reputed to increase sexual desire, have intrigued and captivated human curiosity for centuries. Originating from the name of the Greek goddess of love, Aphrodite, aphrodisiacs have been sought after across various cultures and epochs, woven into the fabric of folklore, medicine, and culinary arts. This section delves into the history, types, and scientific scrutiny surrounding aphrodisiacs, exploring their role in enhancing sexual health and intimacy.

Historically, the use of aphrodisiacs can be traced back to ancient civilizations, which includes the Greeks, Romans, Egyptians, and Chinese, each of whom identified certain foods, drinks, and herbs as capable of increasing sexual desire and potency. These ancient peoples often attributed magical properties to natural substances, intertwining them with rituals and beliefs about fertility, vitality, and love. For instance, the ancient Egyptians valued figs and honey for their supposed libido-enhancing properties, while the Romans documented recipes for love potions and erotic delicacies in their literature.

Aphrodisiacs fall into several categories, based on their nature and mode of action. Natural aphrodisiacs include various foods, herbs, and spices believed to stimulate desire through various mechanisms. Common examples include chocolate, oysters, and ginseng, each revered for its ability to increase libido and sexual function. Chocolate, rich in phenylethylamine and serotonin, is thought to elevate mood and desire, while oysters are high in zinc, a mineral essential for testosterone production and reproductive health. Ginseng, a revered herb in traditional Chinese medicine, is touted for enhancing stamina and sexual function.

In addition to natural substances, synthetic aphrodisiacs have also been developed, often to treat specific sexual health conditions. Pharmaceuticals like sildenafil (Viagra) and tadalafil (Cialis) are designed to address erectile dysfunction, indirectly acting as aphrodisiacs by improving sexual performance and confidence. While these drugs are effective for many, they do not increase libido per se but rather enhance the physiological response to sexual stimulation.

The scientific scrutiny of aphrodisiacs has yielded mixed results, with some studies affirming the libido-enhancing properties of certain substances and others calling for more research. The challenge in evaluating aphrodisiacs lies in the subjective nature of sexual desire and the myriad factors that influence it, including psychological, physiological, and emotional elements. Despite this, the enduring interest in aphrodisiacs underscores a universal desire to enhance sexual health and intimacy.

The psychological aspect of aphrodisiacs is particularly compelling, as belief and expectation can significantly influence sexual experience. The placebo effect, a well-documented phenomenon in which positive outcomes occur due to belief in the efficacy of a treatment, plays a substantial role in the effectiveness of aphrodisiacs for many individuals. This suggests that the power of aphrodisiacs may lie in their physical properties and their ability to inspire desire and confidence through belief and anticipation.

Modern interest in aphrodisiacs reflects a broader cultural and health trend towards natural and holistic approaches to well-being, including sexual health. Many individuals seek out aphrodisiacs not only for their potential physical effects but also as a means of connecting with their partner, exploring sensuality, and enhancing overall intimacy. The use of aphrodisiacs in this context is often part of a larger lifestyle approach that values communication, connection, and the exploration of pleasure.

In conclusion, the fascination with aphrodisiacs spans the spectrum from ancient lore to modern science, reflecting humanity's perennial quest to enhance love, desire, and sexual connection. While scientific evidence varies, the enduring appeal of aphrodisiacs speaks to their perceived value in enhancing sexual experience and intimacy. Whether through the consumption of certain foods and herbs, the use of pharmaceutical aids, or the power of belief and expectation, aphrodisiacs remain a captivating subject of interest for those seeking to enrich their sexual lives. As research continues to explore the potential of these substances, the integration of aphrodisiacs into a balanced and healthy approach to sexuality suggests a continued appreciation for the intricate dance between body, mind, and spirit in the realm of human desire.

Recipes for Love Elixirs and Potions

Throughout history, cultures around the globe have concocted various love elixirs and potions, believed to ignite passion, deepen emotional connections, and summon the elusive forces of love. These concoctions often blend the mystical with the material, weaving together ingredients renowned for their aphrodisiac properties with rituals imbued with intention and desire. This section explores the art of crafting love elixirs and potions, delving into traditional recipes, the significance of their components, and the symbolic rituals surrounding their creation and consumption.

Love potions and elixirs trace their origins to ancient times when healers, shamans, and wise women gathered herbs under the moonlight, whispering intentions and prayers to imbue their concoctions with magical properties. These practices, deeply rooted in the belief in a vibrant, interconnected world where every element holds energy and intention, reflect humanity's enduring quest to influence the realms of love and desire.

One traditional love potion recipe involves blending rose petals, honey, and apple cider vinegar. Roses, long associated with love and the heart, are believed to open the heart chakra, enhancing one's capacity to give and receive love. Honey, with its sweet, nurturing essence, symbolizes the sweetness of love, attracting positive energy and warm feelings. Apple cider vinegar, which is known for its cleansing properties, is said to clear away obstacles and negativity, paving the way for a fresh start or a deepened connection. Combined, these ingredients create a potent elixir that is often shared between lovers or consumed with intention by an individual seeking love.

Another revered recipe hails from the practice of Ayurveda and involves the use of ashwagandha, an adaptogenic herb known for its stress-relieving properties, mixed with warm milk, almond, and saffron. Ashwagandha is believed to balance the energies within the body, fostering emotional stability and vitality—qualities essential for maintaining loving relationships. Almonds, rich in vitamin E, are considered fertility boosters and symbols of enduring passion. Saffron, a rare and precious spice, is thought to enhance libido and sexual energy. This elixir is traditionally consumed before bed, its warming and comforting qualities nurturing the body and soul, preparing the ground for love to flourish.

In Western herbalism, a popular love potion consists of damiana, cacao, and vanilla, mixed into a warm beverage or alcoholic tincture. Damiana, a herb native to the

Americas, is celebrated for its ability to stimulate the senses and enhance sexual desire. Cacao, the source of chocolate, contains compounds that stimulate the brain's pleasure centers, evoking feelings of euphoria and attraction. With its intoxicating aroma, Vanilla is believed to heighten arousal and induce feelings of comfort and joy. This potion, often shared in intimate settings, catalyzes romance and connection, embodying the physical and emotional aspects of love.

The creation and sharing of love elixirs and potions are often accompanied by rituals that enhance their magical properties. These rituals might involve reciting specific intentions or affirmations, lighting candles to invoke the element of fire, or even performing the concoction's preparation and consumption under the auspices of a full moon, believed to amplify magical energies. The power of these rituals lies not only in the ingredients themselves but in the practitioner's focused intention and emotional investment, imbuing the potion with personal significance and energy.

While the efficacy of love elixirs and potions is a matter of belief and personal experience, their significance extends beyond their immediate effects. These concoctions represent a tangible expression of the human desire to connect, love, and be loved. They symbolize the blending of the physical and the mystical, the material and the spiritual, in the quest for one of life's most profound experiences: love.

In contemporary times, the art of crafting love elixirs and potions continues to enchant and inspire. Whether viewed as symbolic gestures, tools for self-reflection and intention-setting, or as means to enhance physical and emotional intimacy, these ancient concoctions remind us of the deep connections between nature, spirituality, and the human heart. As we continue to explore and reinterpret these age-old recipes, we engage in a timeless dialogue about love's nature, its challenges, and its ineffable power to transform our lives.

Herbalism and Sex Magic

Herbalism, the ancient practice of employing plants for healing and spiritual purposes, intersects profoundly with the mystical realm of sex magic, a discipline where sexual energy is harnessed to manifest intentions. This section explores the symbiotic relationship between herbalism and sex magic, illustrating how herbs are employed to enhance sexual vitality, deepen connections, and amplify the magical intentions set forth in sexual rituals.

The roots of using herbs in sex magic stretch back to ancient civilizations, where the natural world was deeply revered and considered imbued with divine energy. Civilizations such as the Egyptians, Greeks, and Romans, along with practitioners of Traditional Chinese Medicine and Ayurveda, all recognized the potent properties of certain herbs to affect the human body and spirit, including aspects of sexual health and emotional well-being. These traditions laid the groundwork for the integration of herbalism into sex magic practices, acknowledging the profound effect that plants can have on the human energetic system, particularly in relation to love, desire, and sexual expression.

At the heart of combining herbalism with sex magic is the understanding that herbs can energetically and physically influence the body's sexual functions and the subtle energies associated with sexual expression. Herbs such as damiana, maca, and ginseng are celebrated for their libido-enhancing properties. Damiana, for instance, has been used for centuries as an aphrodisiac, believed to stimulate sexual desire and increase pleasure. Maca, a root indigenous to the Andes, is reputed to balance hormones and boost stamina, while ginseng is valued for its ability to increase energy and improve sexual function.

Beyond their physiological effects, herbs also play a crucial role in the energetic and symbolic aspects of sex magic. With its connection to love and the heart chakra, Rose is often used in rituals to open the heart and enhance emotional intimacy. Similarly, yarrow is employed for its protective qualities, safeguarding the sacred space and the practitioners from negative influences. Herbs like jasmine and vanilla are incorporated for their sensual aromas, heightening the senses and setting the mood for magical work. The selection of herbs is guided by their correspondences to specific intentions, planetary influences, and elemental energies, creating a harmonious blend that aligns with the ritual's goals.

The application of herbs in sex magic is varied and creative, ranging from burning herbs as incense to cleanse and consecrate the ritual space, to creating herbal oils and elixirs for anointing the body or ingesting before the practice. Bathing in herbal-infused waters is another way to prepare the body and spirit for sex magic, facilitating a deep connection to the plant's energies and the ritual's intentions. Engaging with the herbs—whether through smell, taste, or touch—grounds the practitioner, enhancing their focus and presence in the ritual.

The integration of herbalism into sex magic not only amplifies the potency of the ritual but also fosters a more profound connection to the natural world. It reflects a holistic approach to sexuality and spirituality, where the body is honored as an integral part of the magical practice, and the earth's gifts are revered and utilized with gratitude. This relationship embodies a reciprocal exchange, where the practitioner draws on the plant's energy for magical purposes while also offering respect and care for the plant and its environment.

Moreover, the use of herbs in sex magic reminds us of the interconnectedness of all things. It highlights the belief that the physical and spiritual realms are not separate but deeply intertwined, with the natural world acting as a bridge between the two. Through the conscious use of herbs, practitioners engage in a dialogue with the earth, accessing ancient wisdom and the primal forces of creation inherent in both nature and human sexuality.

In conclusion, herbalism and sex magic share a rich and dynamic relationship, rooted in recognizing the natural world's power to influence and enhance human experience. The use of herbs in sex magic rituals offers a means to deepen intimacy, amplify intentions, and connect with the earth's cycles and energies. This practice underscores the holistic nature of magic and sexuality, where the physical and spiritual merge in the pursuit of transformation, healing, and manifestation. As practitioners continue to explore and honor this connection, they participate in an age-old tradition that celebrates the sacredness of the body, the potency of desire, and the profound wisdom of the plant kingdom.

Safety and Ethical Considerations

The allure of passion potions, concoctions believed to ignite or enhance romantic desire and sexual intimacy, is as old as human history itself. While the intrigue surrounding these elixirs persists in the modern age, it is accompanied by necessary discussions on safety and ethical considerations. This section delves into the critical aspects of exploring passion potions, highlighting the importance of consent, the responsible use of ingredients, and the ethical implications of utilizing such potions in contemporary contexts.

At the forefront of exploring passion potions is the paramount importance of consent. In the context of this discussion, the term "consent" pertains to the agreement to engage in sexual acts upon being fully informed, voluntarily, and enthusiastically. When consuming any substance that is designed to impact desire or sexual experience, all people involved are required to be fully aware of the substance and to give their consent to its intake. The use of passion potions without the explicit consent of all individuals involved not only breaches ethical standards but also legal boundaries, leading to serious consequences. Therefore, the ethical exploration of passion potions begins with a transparent dialogue among participants, ensuring that everyone is making an informed choice.

Another significant safety consideration is the responsible sourcing and use of ingredients in passion potions. Many recipes for these elixirs include herbs, spices, and other natural substances reputed for their aphrodisiac properties. It is essential to have a thorough understanding of the potential effects, both beneficial and adverse, of these ingredients. For instance, some herbs may interact negatively with medications or have contraindications for specific health conditions. Therefore, researching and possibly consulting a healthcare professional or a knowledgeable herbalist before using such substances is advisable. Moreover, sourcing ingredients from reputable suppliers is critical to avoid contamination or adulteration, which could lead to unintended health risks.

The ethical considerations of exploring passion potions extend beyond the immediate health and safety concerns. The intention behind using these potions raises questions about autonomy, manipulation, and the nature of desire. It is ethically problematic to attempt to use a potion to control or alter someone's feelings or actions without their knowledge and consent. Such behavior undermines the principles of respect and autonomy that are foundational to healthy relationships. Ethical exploration of passion potions respects the autonomy of all individuals involved, emphasizing enhancement and exploration within consensual and mutually agreed-upon boundaries.

Moreover, the cultural and historical contexts of certain ingredients and recipes for passion potions warrant respectful consideration. Many potions draw on indigenous knowledge and traditional practices that are deeply rooted in specific cultural contexts. The appropriation of these practices without understanding or respecting their origins and meanings can be ethically problematic. Engaging with these traditions in a way that honors their cultural significance and seeks to understand their historical uses contributes to a more respectful and informed exploration of passion potions.

In addition to ethical considerations, exploring passion potions involves a commitment to personal and mutual well-being. This includes recognizing the limits of such potions' efficacy and understanding that they are not a panacea for relationship issues or sexual dissatisfaction. Open communication, mutual respect, and ongoing consent are essential components of exploring passion potions and sexual intimacy more broadly. The use of these elixirs should be part of a broader context of healthy relationship dynamics, where the emotional and physical well-being of all parties is prioritized.

Exploring passion potions also presents an opportunity for personal growth and exploration within ethical boundaries. When approached with curiosity, respect, and consent, the exploration of aphrodisiacs and elixirs can enhance intimacy and connection between consenting adults. This exploration should be guided by a spirit of mutual care, exploration, and the understanding that true passion and desire cannot be manufactured but can be invited and nurtured.

In conclusion, exploring passion potions is intertwined with complex safety and ethical considerations that demand careful attention. Consent, responsible sourcing, and use of ingredients, respect for cultural practices, and a focus on healthy relationship dynamics are paramount.

When navigated thoughtfully, exploring passion potions offers a unique avenue for enhancing intimacy and connection, rooted in the principles of mutual respect, safety, and ethical integrity. By adhering to these considerations, individuals can explore the realms of desire and intimacy with a conscientious and informed approach.

CHAPTER VI

Love Rituals for Connection

Setting the Mood with Rituals

Rituals have been an integral part of human civilization, bridging the mundane and the sacred, the physical and the spiritual. They mark transitions, celebrate milestones, and, importantly, set the mood for various aspects of life, including those of intimacy and connection. This section delves into the art of setting the mood with rituals, exploring their significance, the elements that comprise them, and their impact on creating an atmosphere conducive to desired outcomes.

The intention behind the action is at the core of using rituals to set the mood. Intention is the guiding force, infusing each ritual element with purpose and direction. Whether the goal is to foster a sense of peace, invoke a feeling of romance, or prepare the space for deeper spiritual connection, the clarity of intention is paramount. This focused intent transforms ordinary actions into meaningful gestures, elevating the atmosphere and aligning the energy of the space with the desired mood.

The elements of rituals that set the mood are varied and rich in symbolism. They often include using candles, whose flickering flames represent the light of consciousness illuminating the darkness of ignorance. Lighting candles can signify the beginning of a sacred time, distinguishing it from the routine of daily life. The colors of the candles further enhance the mood—red for passion and love, white for purity and new beginnings, and black for protection and deep reflection.

Incense and aromatic oils are also pivotal in setting the mood through rituals. The act of burning incense or diffusing oils fills the space with scents that can relax the mind, stimulate the senses, or evoke specific memories and emotions. Lavender, for example, is known for its calming properties, while jasmine and rose are often associated with love and sensuality. The choice of scent is a powerful tool in creating an atmosphere that resonates with the ritual's intention.

Sound, too, plays a critical role in setting the mood. Chanting, drumming, or playing instrumental music can alter the energy of a space, facilitating a shift in awareness and opening the heart and mind to more profound experiences. The vibrations of sound can clear negative energy, harmonize the vibrations within the space, and serve as a focal point for meditation and contemplation.

The physical setting of the ritual is equally important. The choice of location, the arrangement of the space, and the incorporation of natural elements like water, stones, or crystals can significantly impact the mood. A clean, decluttered space invites a flow of positive energy, while the presence of elements from nature connects the participants to the earth and the cycles of life, grounding the ritual in the material and the spiritual world.

Personal adornment and the body's preparation can also be considered elements of rituals that set the mood. Dressing in specific colors or fabrics, anointing the body with oils, or adorning oneself with jewelry charged with intention can enhance the individual's resonance with the ritual's purpose. This preparation helps shift the individual from the ordinary into a state of heightened awareness and readiness for future experiences.

The impact of setting the mood with rituals is profound. These carefully crafted moments create a container for the following experiences, imbuing them with depth, meaning, and intention. By engaging the senses, invoking symbolism, and aligning with the desired energy, rituals can transform ordinary encounters into sacred experiences. They foster a sense of connection to oneself, others, and the broader universe.

Furthermore, rituals that set the mood facilitate psychological and emotional transitions. They signal to the mind and the body that a shift is occurring, preparing the individual to engage with the moment fully. This preparation is essential for deepening intimacy, enhancing spiritual practices, or simply creating a peaceful refuge from the demands of everyday life.

In contemporary society, where the pace of life often leaves little room for pause and reflection, the art of setting the mood with rituals is a powerful antidote. It invites slowness, mindfulness, and a return to the sensual and the experiential. Whether in the context of intimate relationships, personal spiritual practice, or communal celebrations, rituals that set the mood remind us of the beauty and depth that can be found in deliberate, intentional actions.

In conclusion, setting the mood with rituals is a transformative practice that enhances the quality of experiences by imbuing them with intention, symbolism, and depth. Through the mindful selection of elements and the clear articulation of intent, these rituals bridge the mundane and the sacred, creating spaces where profound connection and transformation can occur. As individuals and communities continue to explore and incorporate these practices, they rediscover the power of ritual to mark, celebrate, and deepen the human experience.

Tantric Practices for Intimacy

Tantric practices, rooted in ancient Hindu and Buddhist traditions, offer a profound path to deepen intimacy and connection, transcending the conventional boundaries of physical love to embrace a spiritual union. This section explores the essence of Tantric practices for intimacy, highlighting their philosophical underpinnings, key practices, and their transformative impact on relationships.

At the heart of Tantra is the belief that the divine resides within everything, including the physical body, making every interaction a potential sacred encounter. Unlike many spiritual traditions that seek to transcend the physical realm, Tantra embraces it, viewing sexuality as a vital element of the spiritual journey. This perspective challenges the dichotomy between the spiritual and the physical, proposing that through conscious sexual practices, individuals can experience divine bliss and profound union with the partner and the universe.

Central to Tantric practices for intimacy is cultivating presence and mindful awareness. This involves being fully present with one's partner, where every touch, breath, and gaze is imbued with intention and reverence. The emphasis is on the quality of the connection rather than the pursuit of climax, allowing couples to navigate the depths of their relationship beyond the physical dimension. Through practices such as eye gazing, synchronized breathing, and slow, mindful touch, partners can foster a deep emotional and energetic connection, dissolving barriers and fostering a sense of unity.

Breathwork is another cornerstone of Tantric intimacy. Through various breathing techniques, partners can align their energies, intensify their connection, and enhance their sexual experience. Techniques such as the Harmonizing Breath, where partners breathe together in unison, or the Charging Breath, designed to energize and awaken the body's sexual energy, facilitate a deep, energetic union that transcends the physical act of sex.

Meditation and visualization practices in Tantra serve to heighten intimacy by aligning partners' intentions and focusing their minds on the sacredness of their union. These practices can include visualizing energy moving between the chakras or energy centers, invoking deities of love and passion, or simply meditating on the essence of love and connection. Couples can cultivate a shared sacred space through these spiritual practices, enhancing their relationship's emotional and spiritual depth.

Rituals play a significant role in Tantric intimacy practices, imbuing sexual encounters with a sense of sacredness and purpose. These rituals can range from simple acts, such as lighting candles or creating a beautiful, inviting space, to more elaborate ceremonies involving offerings, prayers, and invading divine energies. By framing their intimate encounters within the ritual context, partners can elevate their experience, creating a bridge between the physical and the divine.

The practice of controlled sexual energy is also pivotal in Tantra. Rather than rushing towards climax, Tantra teaches the art of sublimation and control, where sexual energy is slowly built up and then circulated through the body. This approach not only intensifies pleasure but also transforms sexual energy into a powerful force for spiritual growth and healing. Techniques such as the Valley Orgasm, where partners maintain a high level of arousal without climaxing, encourage a deeper exploration of sexuality, intimacy, and the potential for ecstatic states of consciousness.

The impact of Tantric practices on intimacy is profound. By focusing on the spiritual aspects of sexuality, couples can transcend the limitations of conventional sexual encounters, exploring new dimensions of connection and pleasure. These practices foster a deeper understanding and respect for one's partner, nurturing a bond that is based on mutual reverence, love, and spiritual partnership.

Moreover, Tantric practices for intimacy offer a path to personal transformation. By exploring sexuality as a sacred and spiritual act, individuals can confront and heal deep-seated emotional wounds, release blockages, and embrace a more holistic understanding of themselves and their partners. This journey can lead to greater self-awareness, emotional freedom, and a more fulfilling relationship.

In conclusion, Tantric practices for intimacy offer a rich and transformative path for couples seeking to deepen their connection beyond the physical realm. By embracing the principles of presence, breathwork, meditation, ritual, and controlled sexual energy, partners can explore the sacred dimensions of their relationship, experiencing profound union and spiritual growth. Tantra challenges conventional perceptions of sexuality, offering a vision of intimacy where the divine dances with the physical, and love becomes a gateway to spiritual awakening and union.

Sacred Sexuality and Emotional Bonding

Sacred sexuality transcends the physical act of sex, elevating it to a spiritual experience that fosters deep emotional bonding between partners. This section delves into the concept of sacred sexuality, its foundations, practices, and its profound impact on emotional bonding and intimacy within relationships.

Sacred sexuality is rooted in the belief that sexual union is not merely a physical interaction but a profound communion that can lead to spiritual awakening and deep emotional connections. This perspective sees sexuality as a sacred gift, capable of expressing love, generating life, and accessing spiritual dimensions. Within this framework, sexual energy is recognized as a powerful force for healing, transformation, and the deepening of emotional bonds.

At the heart of sacred sexuality is the intention to honor the divine within oneself and one's partner. This intentionality transforms the sexual act into a ritual of connection, where every touch, kiss, and embrace is imbued with reverence and mindfulness. Such an approach requires open communication, mutual respect, and a deep commitment to exploring the depths of one's own and one's partner's emotional and spiritual landscapes.

Practices within sacred sexuality often involve creating a sacred space for intimacy. This might include setting aside uninterrupted time for one another, creating a comfortable and inviting environment, and perhaps incorporating elements such as candles, music, or incense to enhance the atmosphere. The aim is to step away from the mundane and enter a space where time slows down, allowing partners to fully engage with each other on all levels—physical, emotional, and spiritual.

Breathwork and eye gazing are common techniques used to enhance connection and emotional bonding. By synchronizing breathing and maintaining eye contact, partners can cultivate a sense of unity and empathy, breaking down barriers and promoting a profound sense of being seen and understood. These practices help in aligning energies and intentions, setting the stage for a deeper and more meaningful exchange.

Tantric practices, which are often associated with sacred sexuality, emphasize the slow build-up of sexual energy, mindful touch, and the prolongation of pleasure. Tantra teaches that by delaying gratification and focusing on the journey rather than the destination, partners can experience heightened states of pleasure and intimacy. This approach encourages partners to explore each other's bodies and desires without judgment, creating a safe space for vulnerability and emotional expression.

The impact of sacred sexuality on emotional bonding is significant. By engaging in practices that honor the sacredness of the sexual union, partners can experience a deepening of trust and emotional intimacy. The emphasis on mindfulness, respect, and intentionality helps in creating a strong emotional connection, where both partners feel valued, seen, and connected on a soul level. This form of intimacy transcends physical pleasure, touching the heart of being in a loving, committed relationship.

Furthermore, sacred sexuality offers a pathway for healing past traumas and overcoming inhibitions. By approaching sexuality with reverence and care, individuals can work through emotional blockages and past hurts within the safety of their relationship. This healing process strengthens the bond between partners and contributes to individual growth and self-awareness.

Sacred sexuality also challenges societal norms and misconceptions about sex, proposing a holistic view that celebrates sexuality as an integral part of human experience and spirituality. By embracing this perspective, partners can reject shame and guilt often associated with sexual expression, stepping into a space of freedom and authenticity.

Moreover, sacred sexuality fosters a sense of spiritual connection, both with one's partner and the divine. By recognizing the spiritual dimensions of sexual union, partners can experience a sense of oneness that transcends the physical realm, reinforcing the emotional bond and deepening their commitment to each other.

In conclusion, sacred sexuality is a profound path to deep emotional bonding and intimacy. By honoring the divine within and between partners, engaging in mindful and intentional practices, and creating a space of respect and reverence, couples can transform their sexual union into a powerful vehicle for emotional and spiritual connection. Sacred sexuality invites individuals to explore the depths of their hearts and souls, strengthening their bond and enriching their relationship in ways that resonate far beyond the bedroom. Through this sacred approach to sexuality, partners can discover a wellspring of love, healing, and unity, celebrating the beauty and depth of their connection.

Healing Through Love Rituals

Healing through love rituals is an ancient and transformative practice that recognizes love as a powerful force capable of fostering profound healing, both emotionally and spiritually. Rooted in various cultural traditions and spiritual philosophies, love rituals serve as conduits for deep connection, emotional release, and restoring balance and harmony within the self and in relationships. This section explores the concept of healing through love rituals, detailing their significance, their various forms, and their impact on individuals and communities seeking healing and wholeness.

At the core of love rituals is the understanding that love transcends mere emotion, embodying a universal, healing energy that connects all beings. These rituals harness this energy, directing it toward the healing of heartaches, the mending of broken relationships, or the personal journey toward self-love and acceptance. The practice of love rituals is predicated on the belief that by engaging in intentional acts of love, individuals can tap into a profound source of healing and transformation.

One significant aspect of love rituals is their ability to facilitate emotional release. Many love rituals involve expressions of gratitude, forgiveness, or the verbalization of deep-seated feelings, which can help release pent-up emotions and clear energetic blockages. Such rituals may include writing letters of forgiveness to oneself or others, creating altars dedicated to love and healing, or engaging in meditative practices focused on the heart chakra, the energy center associated with love and compassion.

Another form of love ritual involves the creation of sacred space for intimacy and connection, both with oneself and with others. This can include practices such as sharing meals prepared with intention, participating in couples' meditation or breathwork sessions, or simply spending time in nature together. These rituals foster a sense of presence and mindfulness, allowing individuals and couples to connect on a deeper level, beyond the distractions of daily life.

Self-love rituals are also crucial to healing through love. In a society that often promotes self-criticism and comparison, rituals that celebrate self-acceptance, self-care, and self-compassion can be incredibly healing. Such rituals might involve affirmations of self-worth, self-care practices like baths or body anointing with oils, or creative expression through art or journaling. By honoring oneself through these rituals, individuals can cultivate a loving relationship with themselves, laying the foundation for emotional well-being and resilience.

Community love rituals play a vital role in fostering collective healing and support. These rituals can take many forms, from group meditations focused on sending love and healing to those in need, to community gatherings that celebrate love through dance, music, and shared stories. By coming together in a spirit of love and support, communities can create a powerful collective energy that amplifies the healing process, offering strength and solace to those facing challenges.

The impact of healing through love rituals is profound and multifaceted. On a personal level, these rituals can lead to significant emotional healing, releasing old wounds and fostering a sense of peace and self-love. Love rituals can deepen connections, enhance communication, and resolve conflicts, creating a stronger foundation of trust and understanding. On a communal level, love rituals can unite individuals, promoting empathy, compassion, and a sense of belonging.

Moreover, healing through love rituals contributes to spiritual growth and development. By engaging with the energy of love, individuals can experience a greater sense of connection to the divine, the universe, or whatever higher power they believe in. This spiritual connection can provide comfort, guidance, and a more profound sense of purpose, enriching the individual's journey toward healing and wholeness.

In conclusion, healing through love rituals represents a powerful and holistic approach to emotional and spiritual well-being. Whether practiced alone, with a partner, or within a community, these rituals harness the transformative power of love to heal, connect, and uplift. By intentionally engaging in acts of love, individuals can tap into a universal source of healing, fostering personal growth, deeper relationships, and greater harmony with the world around them. As humanity continues to navigate the complexities of life, the practice of love rituals remains a timeless and essential tool for healing, offering a pathway to a more compassionate, connected, and loving world.

CHAPTER VII

Advanced Techniques and Rituals

Working with Deities and Archetypes

Working with deities and archetypes is a profound spiritual practice that spans various cultures and traditions. It involves connecting with symbolic representations and personifications of universal principles, qualities, and forces of nature, which gods, goddesses, and archetypal figures often embody. This section explores the significance of these practices, their methodologies, and their transformative potential for personal growth and understanding.

The significance of deities and archetypes in spiritual practice lies in their ability to act as mirrors to the human psyche, reflecting deep truths about the nature of existence, the human condition, and the journey of the soul. Deities, revered in religious and mythological traditions, encapsulate the multifaceted aspects of life and the cosmos, offering pathways to understanding and relating to the world's inherent sacredness. Similarly, archetypes, a concept popularized by psychologist Carl Jung, represent universal patterns of behavior and experience residing in the collective unconscious. Working with these figures facilitates a dialogue with the deeper layers of the self and the universal narratives that shape human experience.

The methodology of working with deities and archetypes varies, often involving ritual, meditation, study, and creative expression. Practitioners might choose a particular deity or archetype to work with based on personal affinity, the qualities or support they seek, or guidance received through divination or introspection. Establishing a connection typically involves creating sacred space, including altars adorned with symbols, images, or items associated with the chosen figure. Ritual acts, such as offering prayers, lighting candles, or presenting offerings, are performed to honor the deity or archetype and to invite their presence and influence.

Meditation and visualization techniques are also employed to facilitate a deeper connection. Practitioners might meditate on the symbolism associated with a deity or archetype, envisioning interactions that allow for the exchange of wisdom, guidance, or healing energy. These meditative practices can lead to profound insights, emotional catharsis, and a strengthened sense of purpose and direction.

Studying myths, stories, and attributes associated with deities and archetypes provides further avenues for exploration and understanding. Delving into the lore surrounding these figures can illuminate the lessons they embody, offering valuable perspectives on navigating life's challenges and embracing one's potential. Creative expression, such as writing, art, or dance, inspired by interactions with deities and archetypes, can also be a powerful tool for integrating and manifesting the insights gained.

The impact of working with deities and archetypes on personal growth and spirituality is significant. These practices encourage self-reflection, helping individuals to uncover hidden aspects of their psyche, heal psychological wounds, and transcend limiting beliefs. By aligning with the qualities and strengths of these figures, practitioners can embody their virtues, cultivate resilience, and foster a deeper connection to the sacred aspects of life.

Furthermore, working with deities and archetypes facilitates a sense of belonging and connection to a larger story. It reminds practitioners that they are part of a vast, interconnected cosmos, woven into the fabric of a rich tapestry of myths, symbols, and archetypal energies that span cultures and epochs. This realization can promote a sense of unity, compassion, and empathy for oneself and the collective human experience.

Moreover, these practices offer a framework for understanding and navigating the cycles and seasons of life. Deities and archetypes often represent specific phases of life, transitions, and universal themes, providing guidance and support through life's inevitable changes and challenges. Individuals can draw upon ancient wisdom and archetypal energies by engaging with these figures to navigate their personal journey with greater awareness and intention.

In conclusion, working with deities and archetypes is a deeply enriching practice that bridges the personal with the universal, offering pathways to self-discovery, healing, and spiritual growth. Through ritual, meditation, study, and creative expression, practitioners can connect with the profound wisdom embodied by these figures, gaining insights and support for their life's journey. As a practice rooted in recognizing the interconnectedness of all aspects of existence, working with deities and archetypes encourages a holistic approach to spirituality, where the sacred is found within the self, in others, and in the world at large. This approach fosters a life lived with depth, purpose, and a heartfelt connection to the divine tapestry of existence.

Sacred Symbols and Sigils in Sex Magic

Sacred symbols and sigils have been integral to spiritual and magical practices across cultures and eras, embodying profound meanings and serving as conduits for intention, energy, and transformation. In the realm of sex magic, these symbols and sigils are employed with the belief that they can significantly enhance the potency of rituals, deepen connections, and facilitate the manifestation of desires. This section delves into the use of sacred symbols and sigils in sex magic, exploring their historical roots, methods of creation and use, and their impact on the practice.

The historical roots of using symbols in magical practices are able to be traced back to ancient civilizations, where symbols were believed to hold the essence of gods, cosmic truths, and the fundamental forces of nature. Similarly, sigils—magical symbols created for specific intentions—are a more recent development but draw on the same foundational belief in the power of visual representation to affect reality. In sex magic, these symbols and sigils are not mere decorations but are considered active tools that embody specific energies or goals, aiding practitioners in focusing their intentions and channeling sexual energy towards the desired outcome.

Creating sigils for use in sex magic often involves a process of distilling a written statement of intent into a unique symbol that captures the essence of the desire. This can be done by combining letters, using numerology, or intuitively designing a symbol that resonates with the practitioner's intention. The creation of the sigil itself is a ritual, requiring a clear focus and a meditative state, imbuing the symbol with personal energy and significance. On the other hand, sacred symbols may be drawn from traditional systems such as alchemy, astrology, or any cultural or spiritual tradition that holds meaning for the practitioner. These might include symbols representing divine feminine and masculine energies, the union of opposites, or fertility and abundance.

The use of these symbols and sigils in sex magic is varied and imaginative. They can be inscribed on candles, drawn on the body, visualized during meditation, or placed within the ritual space to create a charged atmosphere. When used in conjunction with sexual energy—considered one of the most potent forces for manifestation—the symbols and sigils act as focal points, concentrating intention and aiding in the visualization process. This focused energy, amplified by the sexual act or sexual arousal, is believed to imprint the practitioner's desires onto the fabric of reality, facilitating their manifestation.

The impact of incorporating sacred symbols and sigils in sex magic is profound. On a psychological level, these symbols can deeply affect the subconscious, serving as constant reminders of the practitioner's intent and reinforcing their focus and commitment to the ritual. The symbolic act of creating and using these sigils and symbols also demarcates the sacred space and time of the ritual from ordinary life, helping practitioners shift into a heightened state of awareness where profound transformation and connection can occur.

Furthermore, the use of symbols and sigils in sex magic fosters a deeper connection to the symbolic language of the unconscious mind, where archetypes and mythic narratives reside. By engaging with this language, practitioners can tap into universal patterns of human experience and the collective unconscious, drawing on its power to inform and energize their personal intentions.

The practice also connects individuals to a long lineage of spiritual seekers, magicians, and mystics who have used symbolic language to explore the mysteries of existence. This connection can provide a sense of continuity, belonging, and wisdom that transcends time and culture, enriching the practitioner's experience and understanding of their own spiritual journey.

In contemporary practice, the use of sacred symbols and sigils in sex magic is a testament to the enduring human belief in the power of intention, symbolism, and the transformative potential of sexual energy. It reflects a holistic view of sexuality as not merely a physical act but a sacred ritual capable of spiritual growth and manifestation. Through the intentional use of symbols and sigils, practitioners can explore the depths of their desires, intentions, and spiritual connections, using sex magic as a potent tool for personal and collective transformation.

In conclusion, sacred symbols and sigils play a crucial role in the practice of sex magic, serving as potent tools for focusing intention, channeling energy, and facilitating manifestation. Their use bridges the physical, spiritual, personal, and universal, drawing on ancient traditions and contemporary insights to enrich the magical work. By engaging with these symbols, practitioners can deepen their connection to the mystical forces of existence, exploring the sacred dimensions of sexuality and harnessing its power for healing, growth, and transformation.

Group Rituals and Community Practices

Group rituals and community practices in sex magic represent a profound exploration of collective energy, intention, and transformation. Rooted in ancient traditions yet evolving within modern contexts, these communal activities extend beyond individual practice, harnessing the power of collective focus to achieve heightened states of consciousness and manifest shared goals. This section delves into the intricacies of group rituals and community practices within sex magic, their historical roots, methodologies, and their profound impact on participants and the broader community.

Historically, sex magic has been practiced within various cultural and spiritual traditions, often within the context of rites and ceremonies designed to honor deities, celebrate fertility, or invoke divine energies. These communal rituals served as a bridge between the earthly and the divine, leveraging sexual energy as a potent force for spiritual connection, communal bonding, and the manifestation of collective intentions. From the ancient fertility rites of Mesopotamia and Egypt to the tantric practices of Hinduism and Buddhism, the communal aspect of sex magic has been integral to its practice, emphasizing the interconnectedness of all beings and the sacredness of sexual energy.

In modern group rituals and community practices of sex magic, a diversity of approaches can be observed, ranging from ceremonial gatherings focused on specific intentions to workshops and retreats designed to explore and deepen understanding of sexual energy as a tool for spiritual growth and manifestation. These practices are often grounded in principles of consent, mutual respect, and ethical engagement, ensuring a safe and supportive environment for all participants.

A key component of group rituals in sex magic is the establishment of a sacred space, which may involve the creation of altars, the use of symbolic objects, and the invocation of protective energies. The space is consecrated through rituals, including chanting, drumming, and using sacred symbols, creating a container for the work to unfold. Within this sacred space, participants engage in practices designed to raise and harmonize sexual energy, such as synchronized breathing, movement, and visualization exercises. The collective focus and energy of the group serve to amplify the intention of the ritual, creating a powerful vortex for manifestation.

The methodologies employed in group rituals and community practices of sex magic are diverse, reflecting the unique intentions and cultural backgrounds of the participants. Some rituals may involve partnered exercises designed to explore and exchange energy, while others may focus on solo practices within the collective setting, respecting individual boundaries and preferences. Central to these methodologies is cultivating a deep, empathic connection among participants, fostering a sense of unity and mutual support.

The impact of participating in group rituals and community practices of sex magic is multifaceted. On an individual level, these practices can lead to profound personal insights, healing, and transformation, deepening one's connection to their sexual and spiritual selves. The collective aspect of the rituals can strengthen the sense of community and belonging, creating bonds that extend beyond the ritual space. For the broader community, these practices can catalyze cultural shifts, challenging prevailing norms around sexuality and spirituality and promoting a more integrated, holistic understanding of sexual energy.

Moreover, group rituals and community practices in sex magic can contribute to collective healing, addressing wounds related to sexuality, power, and connection. By engaging in these rituals, participants can experience a reclamation of sexual agency, empowerment, and the healing of trauma, both individually and collectively. These practices offer a space for expressing vulnerability and strength, inviting transformation at both personal and communal levels.

Ethical considerations are paramount in group rituals and community practices of sex magic. The principles of consent, transparency, and respect are foundational, ensuring that all participants feel safe, honored, and valued. Ethical facilitation involves clear communication of intentions, boundaries, and the structure of the ritual, as well as ongoing attention to the dynamics and needs of the group.

In conclusion, group rituals and community practices in sex magic represent a powerful exploration of collective energy and intention, rooted in ancient traditions yet dynamically engaging with modern contexts. These communal practices offer profound opportunities for spiritual growth, manifestation, and healing, grounded in the sacredness of sexual energy. By fostering deep connections, ethical engagement, and a shared focus on transformation, group rituals in sex magic contribute to the evolution of individual and collective consciousness, embodying the potential for profound change and realizing collective aspirations. Through these practices, communities can navigate the complexities of human experience, embracing the transformative power of sexual energy as a force for healing, connection, and spiritual awakening.

Exploring Ecstatic States and Beyond

Exploring ecstatic states transcends the boundaries of ordinary consciousness, offering profound insights into the nature of existence, the self, and the universe. Ecstatic experiences, characterized by intense feelings of joy, transcendence, and a deep sense of connection, have been sought after and revered across various cultures and spiritual traditions. This section delves into the nature of ecstatic states, the methods by which individuals and communities seek them, and the transformative impact these experiences can have on personal growth and understanding.

At the heart of the quest for ecstatic states is a universal human desire to experience greater connection and understanding. Ecstatic states are moments where the self dissolves, and a profound unity with all that is, becomes palpable. These experiences often carry a sense of ineffability, transcending the limitations of language and conventional thought. They can be spontaneous or induced through various practices and disciplines, reflecting the diverse paths humanity has explored in its quest for transcendence.

Various spiritual traditions and practices have evolved to facilitate the attainment of ecstatic states. In Sufism, the mystical branch of Islam, practices such as whirling, chanting, and meditation are pathways to ecstatic experiences of divine love and union. Similarly, in Hinduism and Buddhism, techniques like deep meditation, chanting of mantras, and yogic practices are employed to transcend ordinary consciousness and attain states of bliss and enlightenment.

Shamanic traditions worldwide utilize rhythmic drumming, dance, and the use of entheogens—psychoactive substances used in a religious or spiritual context—to induce ecstatic states. These practices are often part of healing rituals, vision quests, and ceremonies designed to facilitate communication with the spirit world, access deep wisdom, and bring about transformation and healing.

In contemporary times, the exploration of ecstatic states extends into the realms of psychology and neuroscience, with research into practices like meditation, breathwork, and the responsible use of psychedelics. These studies seek to understand the mechanisms behind ecstatic experiences, their potential therapeutic benefits, and their role in fostering creativity, empathy, and a sense of connectedness.

The methods for exploring ecstatic states vary widely, reflecting the rich tapestry of human culture as well as spirituality. Common to many of these practices is the principle of altering ordinary patterns of consciousness—whether through movement, sound, breath, or the ingestion of substances—to open the door to transcendent experiences. These methods are often accompanied by preparatory practices, rituals, and the guidance of experienced practitioners, ensuring safety and enhancing the depth of the experience.

The impact of ecstatic states on individuals is profound and multifaceted. These experiences can lead to significant personal growth, offering insights into one's true nature, dissolving ego-boundaries, and fostering a deep sense of peace and contentment. Many who experience ecstatic states report a lasting sense of connection to something greater than themselves, whether described as the divine, the universe, or the interconnected web of life. This sense of connection can foster a profound empathy for others and a renewed sense of purpose and meaning in life.

Moreover, ecstatic experiences can transform one's understanding of death, suffering, and the mysteries of existence. By transcending the fear of death and glimpsing the unity underlying apparent separateness, individuals can cultivate a more accepting and compassionate approach to life's challenges. This transformation often leads to a reevaluation of values and priorities, guiding individuals toward lives that reflect a deeper understanding of love, service, and the sacredness of existence.

On a communal level, shared ecstatic experiences can strengthen bonds, foster a sense of unity, and facilitate collective healing and celebration. Throughout history, communal rituals involving ecstatic practices have served as vital components of cultural identity, social cohesion, and spiritual nourishment. In contemporary society, gatherings that facilitate ecstatic experiences, such as music and dance festivals, meditation retreats, and group ceremonies, continue to play a significant role in community building and spiritual exploration.

Ethical considerations are paramount in the pursuit of ecstatic states, especially in contexts involving the guidance of others or the use of psychoactive substances. The importance of consent, respect for individual boundaries, and the responsible use of power cannot be overstated. Ensuring that practices are conducted safely, with reverence for the traditions from which they arise and consideration for the well-being of all participants, is essential.

In conclusion, exploring ecstatic states represents a profound human endeavor to transcend the limitations of ordinary consciousness and connect with the deeper realities of existence. Through various practices and within diverse cultural and spiritual frameworks, individuals and communities seek these experiences of unity, transcendence, and deep joy. The quest for ecstatic states, grounded in ethical and mindful exploration, offers pathways to profound personal and collective transformation, inviting a deeper engagement with the mysteries of life and the potential for profound healing and growth.

CHAPTER VIII

Integrating Sex Magic into Daily Life

Maintaining Balance and Harmony

Integrating sex magic into daily life is a profound practice that transcends the boundaries of traditional sexuality, infusing one's existence with intention, energy, and a deeper connection to the universal life force. However, this integration requires a delicate balance and harmony to ensure that it enhances personal growth, relationships, and spiritual journey without causing imbalance or discord. This section explores the methodologies, considerations, and impacts of incorporating sex magic into daily routines, emphasizing the importance of maintaining balance and harmony.

A fundamental tenet of sex magic is the conviction that sexual energy is a potent tool that may be used for the sake of creation, transformation, and manifestation. Harnessing this energy through intention and ritualistic practices can significantly impact one's reality, influencing personal desires, aspirations, and spiritual evolution. Having a knowledge of the sacred nature of sex magic and approaching it with regard, respect, and mindfulness is the most important factor in achieving successful integration.

Methodologies for integrating sex magic into daily life vary, reflecting the diversity of individual paths and practices. For some, it may involve daily meditations focusing on intentions and visualizing desires manifesting through the power of sexual energy. Others may incorporate ritualistic practices into their sexual activities, whether solo or with a partner, setting intentions and using visualization, breathwork, and symbolic objects to direct energy toward desired outcomes. Additionally, the mindful cultivation of sexual energy throughout the day, through practices such as tantra or qigong, can prepare the practitioner for more intentional use of this energy in ritualistic contexts.

Maintaining balance and harmony requires several key considerations. First, the ethical dimension of sex magic cannot be overstated. This involves ensuring that all practices, especially those involving partners, are grounded in consent, communication, and mutual respect. Ethical practice also entails the responsible use of sexual energy, directing it towards positive, constructive outcomes that do not harm oneself or others.

Another critical consideration is the balance between the spiritual and the mundane. While sex magic can elevate sexual activities to spiritual experiences, it is vital to maintain a connection to the grounded, everyday aspects of sexuality and relationships. This balance ensures that sex magic enriches the practitioner's life, enhancing intimacy and connection without overshadowing or neglecting the foundational elements of healthy relationships and sexuality.

The integration of sex magic into daily life also requires mindfulness of one's energy levels and emotional state. Engaging in sex magic can be energetically demanding, necessitating awareness of one's boundaries and the need for rest and recuperation. Practitioners must tune into their bodies and emotions, recognizing when to engage in energetic practices and when to rest, ensuring that their pursuit of spiritual and magical goals remains in harmony with their overall well-being.

The impact of integrating sex magic into daily life can be profound, influencing various aspects of one's existence. On a personal level, regular engagement with sex magic can lead to increased self-awareness, empowerment, and a deeper understanding of one's desires and creative potential. It can also enhance one's connection to the divine or the universal energy that pervades all things, fostering a sense of unity and purpose.

In relationships, the mindful use of sex magic can deepen intimacy, communication, and mutual understanding. By approaching sexual interactions with intention and reverence, partners can explore new dimensions of their connection, experiencing heightened levels of trust, pleasure, and spiritual communion. This deepened connection can spill over into other areas of life, strengthening the bond between partners and enhancing their shared journey.

In addition, the incorporation of sex magic into daily routines has the potential to have a domino impact on the larger community as well as the entire world. As individuals harness their sexual energy for healing, manifestation, and spiritual growth, they contribute to a collective elevation of consciousness. Through their intentions and actions, practitioners of sex magic can influence the energetic fabric of their environment, promoting harmony, love, and transformation on a larger scale.

In conclusion, integrating sex magic into daily life offers a pathway to profound personal growth, deeper relationships, and spiritual evolution. However, this integration requires a commitment to balance, ethical practice, and mindfulness of one's energy and emotional state. By approaching sex magic with reverence, respect, and a desire for positive transformation, practitioners can harness this potent force in a way that enriches their lives and contributes to the greater good. As with any potent tool, the key lies in mindful application, ensuring that the sacredness of sex magic is honored and that its integration into daily life fosters balance, harmony, and holistic well-being.

Incorporating Sex Magic into Relationships

Incorporating sex magic into relationships offers couples a unique pathway to deepen their connection, enhance intimacy, and collectively pursue spiritual growth and manifestation goals. This practice, which combines the potent energy of sexuality with focused intention and ritual, can transform a relationship's dynamics, imbuing it with a deeper sense of purpose, understanding, and unity. This section explores the nuances of integrating sex magic into relationships, covering its foundations, methodologies, and the profound impacts it can have on partnership dynamics.

The foundation of incorporating sex magic into relationships rests on mutual respect, open communication, and a shared interest in exploring the spiritual dimensions of sexuality. It begins with an understanding that sexual energy is not merely for physical gratification but is a powerful force that, when harnessed with intention, can foster profound emotional healing, personal transformation, and the realization of shared desires or goals. For couples, this realization opens up new avenues for connection, allowing them to engage with each other on a deeply spiritual level.

Methodologies for incorporating sex magic into relationships vary, reflecting the unique dynamics of each partnership. A crucial first step is establishing clear intentions, which involves open and honest communication about each partner's desires, boundaries, and spiritual beliefs. This collaborative process ensures that both individuals are aligned in their goals and comfortable with the practices they choose to explore.

One common methodology is the creation of shared rituals, which might include setting up a sacred space, meditating together, engaging in synchronized breathing exercises, or chanting mantras. These rituals serve to elevate the act of sex from the mundane to the sacred, focusing the couple's collective energy and intention. The use of symbols, sigils, or objects that hold personal significance to the couple can also be integrated into these rituals, acting as focal points for their intentions.

Visualization techniques are another vital component, where both partners visualize their combined energy manifesting their intentions. This could be related to deepening their bond, achieving personal or mutual goals, or sending healing energy to areas of their relationship or individual selves that require it. The climax of sexual activity, regarded in sex magic as a potent moment for energy release and manifestation, becomes a powerful tool for bringing these visualized intentions to fruition.

The impact of incorporating sex magic into relationships can be profound. On an emotional level, it fosters a deeper sense of empathy and understanding between partners. Engaging in shared spiritual and magical practices can reveal vulnerabilities and strengths, encouraging a level of openness and trust that strengthens the emotional foundation of the relationship. This process can also lead to significant personal growth for each individual, as they explore their desires, fears, and the power of their sexual energy within a supportive partnership.

Sex magic also enhances sexual satisfaction and intimacy. By approaching sex with intention and reverence, couples can experience heightened pleasure and connection. The focus on energy exchange, rather than solely on physical sensations, can introduce new dimensions to sexual encounters, making them more fulfilling and spiritually significant.

Furthermore, incorporating sex magic into relationships can have a transformative effect on how couples navigate challenges and conflicts. The concepts of mutual respect, open communication, and shared intentionality that underpin sex magic practices can also inform conflict resolution, promoting understanding and compromise. The spiritual bond forged through sex magic can serve as a resilient foundation for navigating the ups and downs of life together.

However, ethical considerations are paramount. Both partners must fully consent to and feel comfortable with incorporating sex magic into their relationship. It's crucial that no partner feels coerced or pressured into participation. The practices chosen should be respectful of each partner's boundaries and beliefs, with ongoing communication to ensure that both individuals remain aligned and comfortable with the process.

In conclusion, incorporating sex magic into relationships offers couples a pathway to explore the deeper spiritual dimensions of their connection, enhance intimacy, foster personal and mutual growth, and manifest shared goals. This practice requires a foundation of trust, open communication, and shared intentions. When approached with respect, love, and ethical consideration, sex magic can profoundly enrich a relationship, offering a unique avenue for couples to explore the sacredness of their union and the transformative power of their combined energies.

Self-Care and Reflection

Incorporating sex magic into one's spiritual practice is a profound journey that extends beyond the boundaries of traditional sexuality, delving into the realms of personal empowerment, manifestation, and self-transformation. This journey, while enriching, also necessitates a commitment to self-care and reflection, ensuring that the practice remains balanced, ethical, and aligned with one's personal growth and well-being. This section explores the significance of self-care and reflection in incorporating sex magic, offering insights into the methodologies, challenges, and transformative potentials of this deeply personal spiritual practice.

Self-care in the context of sex magic is multifaceted, encompassing physical, emotional, and spiritual dimensions. Physically, it involves attending to the body's needs and recognizing that engaging with sexual energy in a ritualistic context can be both energetically demanding and profoundly rejuvenating. Adequate rest, nourishment, and grounding practices become essential, ensuring that the body remains a strong, resilient vessel for the potent energies at play. Emotionally, self-care entails maintaining a compassionate and non-judgmental space for oneself, especially as sex magic can unearth deep-seated emotions, desires, and vulnerabilities. Spiritually, self-care involves regular cleansing and protective rituals to maintain energetic hygiene, safeguarding one's spiritual integrity and ensuring that the connections forged through sex magic are healthy and supportive.

Reflection is equally critical in the practice of sex magic. It provides a space to process experiences, discern lessons, and integrate insights gained through the practice. Reflection can take many forms, including journaling, meditation, or dialogues with trusted mentors or peers in the spiritual community. Through reflection, practitioners can examine their intentions, the outcomes of their rituals, and the personal growth or challenges encountered, allowing for a deeper understanding of the practice's role in their spiritual journey.

Methodologies for integrating self-care and reflection into sex magic are varied and personalized. Establishing a pre-ritual routine that includes setting clear intentions, grounding and centering exercises, and protective visualizations can prepare the practitioner physically and spiritually, creating a foundation of safety and focus. Post-ritual practices might include journaling to record experiences and insights, baths or showers to cleanse and release residual energies, and grounding exercises to reconnect with the physical world. Regularly scheduled periods for reflection, such as weekly or monthly check- ins with oneself or with a spiritual advisor, can provide ongoing support and guidance.

The challenges of incorporating sex magic with attention to self-care and reflection are not insignificant. Navigating the powerful energies of sex magic requires discernment and responsibility, ensuring that one's practices remain aligned with personal ethics and the highest good. The intensity of the experiences may also necessitate confronting personal shadows, past traumas, or unresolved emotional issues, requiring courage and a commitment to healing. Furthermore, the societal stigma surrounding sexuality and magic can present external challenges, including isolation or misunderstanding from others not aligned with or supportive of these practices.

Despite these challenges, the transformative potential of incorporating sex magic with self-care and reflection is immense. Practitioners can experience profound personal growth, including increased self-awareness, empowerment, and a deeper connection to their divine essence. Relationships with others can become more authentic and meaningful, as practitioners bring a heightened sense of self-knowledge and intentionality to their interactions. Moreover, the practice can lead to significant manifestations, aligning the practitioner's reality more closely with their desires and spiritual path.

Self-care and reflection also foster a sustainable practice, ensuring that sex magic remains a source of empowerment and renewal rather than depletion or imbalance. By prioritizing these aspects, practitioners can navigate the challenges and intensities of sex magic with resilience and wisdom, turning potential obstacles into opportunities for growth and healing.

In conclusion, the integration of self-care and reflection into the practice of sex magic is crucial for maintaining balance, ethical integrity, and personal well-being. These practices offer a framework for navigating the profound energies and experiences encountered in sex magic, ensuring that the journey is transformative, sustainable, and aligned with one's highest good. Through dedicated self-care and reflective practices, individuals can explore the depths of their sexual and spiritual selves, unlocking new dimensions of empowerment, manifestation, and personal growth.

Continuing the Journey

The journey in sex magic is a continuous exploration of the self, the universe, and the intricate dance between them, mediated by the potent force of sexual energy. This path, characterized by growth, transformation, and the pursuit of deeper understanding, invites practitioners into an ever-evolving relationship with their sexuality, spirituality, and the manifestation of their deepest desires. This section delves into the aspects of continuing the journey in sex magic, highlighting the importance of evolution, challenges, and the eternal quest for balance and integration.

The evolution of one's practice in sex magic is both a personal and universal journey. As practitioners deepen their understanding of sex magic, they often encounter new layers of complexity within themselves and the practice. This evolution can involve expanding one's knowledge of different traditions and techniques, experimenting with new rituals, and continually refining intentions based on personal growth and changing life circumstances. The journey is non-linear, characterized by learning, experiencing, reflecting, and integrating cycles, allowing for a dynamic and responsive practice that evolves with the practitioner's spiritual path.

A critical aspect of continuing the journey in sex magic is the acknowledgment and embrace of challenges as opportunities for growth. Practitioners may encounter internal challenges, such as confronting deeply held beliefs, fears, or shadows that arise during their work with sexual energy. External challenges can also surface, including navigating societal stigmas around sexuality and magic, or finding community and support in a practice that is often misunderstood or marginalized. These challenges require courage, resilience, and a commitment to personal truth and integrity.

The quest for balance and integration is central to the journey in sex magic. This balance involves harmonizing the spiritual and the physical, the sacred and the mundane, ensuring that the practice enhances all areas of life. Integration speaks to weaving insights and transformations gained through sex magic into daily existence, allowing the practice to inform how one engages with the world, relationships, and personal aspirations. Achieving this balance and integration necessitates ongoing self-reflection, adaptation, and a conscious effort to ground spiritual experiences into tangible actions and choices.

Continuing the journey in sex magic also involves a deepening commitment to ethical practice. As the power of sex magic becomes more apparent, so too does the responsibility to wield this power with respect, consent, and consideration for the well-being of all involved. Ethical practice extends beyond personal rituals to include how practitioners engage with others, share their knowledge, and contribute to the broader community of sex magic practitioners. This commitment to ethics ensures that the practice remains a force for positive transformation, healing, and empowerment.

Community is significant in the ongoing journey in sex magic. Finding or creating supportive communities where experiences, challenges, and insights can be shared is invaluable. These communities offer a space for validation, learning, and growth, providing practitioners with a sense of belonging and connection. Community can be found in various forms, from online forums and also social media groups to local gatherings and workshops, each offering different avenues for connection and exchange.

The personal and collective benefits of continuing the journey in sex magic are profound. On a personal level, practitioners can experience ongoing personal transformation, deeper self-awareness, and an enhanced capacity for joy, pleasure, and fulfillment. Relationships can become more authentic and spiritually connected, enriched by the principles and practices of sex magic. Collectively, the continued exploration of sex magic contributes to a broader cultural shift toward a more open, respectful, and integrated understanding of sexuality and spirituality.

In conclusion, continuing the journey in sex magic is an ever-unfolding path of exploration, transformation, and integration. It invites practitioners into a deeper engagement with the mysteries of existence, the power of sexual energy, and the potential for personal and collective evolution. Through ongoing learning, facing challenges, striving for balance and ethical integrity, and connecting with community, individuals can navigate this journey with wisdom, joy, and a profound sense of purpose. As the practice of sex magic evolves, so too does its capacity to illuminate the sacredness of sexuality, the potential for manifestation, and the interconnectedness of all life.

CHAPTER IX

Reflection

Recap of Key Concepts

The intricate tapestry that is the human experience is brought to light via the investigation of a wide range of significant issues that fall under the categories of spirituality, personal development, and the mystery of sexual energy. The purpose of this section is to provide a summary of important ideas by bringing together the various aspects of sacred sexuality, the transformational power of rituals, the significance of dealing with deities and archetypes, and the incorporation of profound practices into everyday life and interpersonal interactions. Individuals are invited to start on a journey of discovery, healing, and transcendence through each thought, which at the same time is different and interdependent.

In this approach, sacred sexuality emerges as a foundational concept, revealing sexuality not just as a physical act but also as a gateway to spiritual enlightenment and connection. It highlights the power of sexual energy as a force that may bring about profound emotional bonding, personal transformation, and the actualization of desires. Sacred sexuality is a way that transcends traditional ideas of sexuality and offers a road where the act of love becomes a ritual of union with the divine. This path fosters a greater understanding of one's spiritual identity as well as the interconnectedness of all things.

This underscores the human tendency to create sacred locations and moments that transcend the everyday, which is shown by the role of rituals in enriching both individual and collective experiences. In the context of sex magic, community meetings, or personal spiritual practices, rituals serve as vehicles for intention, transformation, and the nurturing of deeper relationships. This is true regardless of the environment in which the ritual is performed. They are a representation of the power that symbolic gestures have to bring about change, to embody intentions, and to honor the sacredness of the journey that is my life.

The concept of engaging with symbolic representations of universal energies and principles is introduced through the process of working with deities and archetypes. Through the use of this practice, individuals are able to access the collective unconscious, drawing on archetypal patterns and divine energies in order to get guidance, empowerment, and understanding. Through the establishment of relationships with these figures, practitioners are able to navigate the complexities of their inner landscapes, so gaining insights into their behavior, desires, and the purpose of their lives. By engaging in this activity, one is able to cultivate a conversation with the more profound aspects of oneself and the universe, so enhancing the spiritual path with mythic dimensions and transforming energies.

The infusion of sex magic into day-to-day living and relationships places an emphasis on the practical application of spiritual practices in the process of promoting personal development, intimacy, and the realization of goals. Not only does it emphasize the significance of intentionality and ethical practice, but it also emphasizes the growth of a sacred orientation to sexuality. Individuals and couples have the ability to harness the creative power of sexual energy by incorporating sex magic into their life. This allows them to strengthen their emotional bonds and spiritual connections, as well as actively co-create their reality in a manner that is congruent with their most profound ambitions.

When it comes to maintaining a balanced as well as healthy involvement with significant spiritual practices, self-care and introspection emerge as key factors that must be considered. They emphasize the significance of paying attention to the physical, emotional, and spiritual well-being of practitioners. This is done to guarantee that the investigation of profound energies and practices that are transforming continues to be nourishing and affirming of life. Individuals are able to analyze their experiences, gain knowledge from their journeys, and make conscious decisions that are in alignment with their highest good when they engage in thoughtful reflection, which serves as a tool for integration and comprehension.

In the realm of sex magic, the trip is marked by ongoing development, the pursuit of balance, and the encounter with challenges. By providing practitioners with opportunities to undergo profound personal and collective transformations, it encourages practitioners to engage in an ongoing examination of their sexuality and spirituality. This path involves a dedication to ethical practice, self-awareness, and the building of supporting networks. It also requires the creation of an environment that allows for the sacred potential of sexual energy to be explored with wisdom and integrity.

By reviewing these fundamental ideas, it becomes clear that the investigation of sacred sexuality, rituals, deities, and archetypes, as well as the incorporation of meaningful practices into one's daily life, is a holistic route that leads to enlightenment and fulfillment. On this path, individuals are challenged to go beyond their limitations, accept their power, and establish a profound connection with the secrets of creation. As a result of this journey, the potential for healing, empowerment, and unification with the divine becomes not merely a possibility but a lived reality, so enriching the fabric of human experience with a more profound sense of meaning, purpose, and connection.

Encouragement for Further Exploration

The exploration of the worlds of spirituality, personal development, and the mystical aspects of existence is a journey that is both profound and expansive. The challenge it poses to individuals is to investigate the intricacies of their own existence as well as the secrets of the universe. It encourages people to go beyond what they are familiar with. This section is meant to serve as a call to action for further investigation, drawing attention to the countless chances for personal development, comprehension, and interpersonal connection that are waiting for those who are willing to go further.

Taking the first step toward deeper discovery calls for bravery, curiosity, and a heart that is open to new experiences. Those that seek with sincerity and openness will find that the cosmos is a treasure trove of knowledge that is just waiting to be uncovered. No matter if it is through the study of old spiritual traditions, the practice of meditation and mindfulness, or the investigation of one's inner worlds, the trip is characterized by an infinite number of opportunities for learning and expansion. New vistas are opened up with each step that is taken, providing insights into the essence of reality, the interconnectedness of all life, and the potential for profound human development.

Both the call to embrace the unknown and the encouragement to explore more are included in this invitation. The route of spiritual inquiry is not a linear one; rather, it is a journey that frequently goes into new places, both externally and internally. The willingness to let go of previous assumptions and to approach each event with the mindset of a beginner is necessary in order to embrace the unknown. The most profound discoveries are produced in the space of not knowing, exposing new parts of the self and the cosmos that were before concealed from view. This is the space in which the most extraordinary discoveries are made.

Further inquiry necessitates a profound dedication to one's own personal development as well. It places individuals in a position where they are forced to confront their shadows, heal old wounds, and transcend limiting beliefs. It is vital for individuals to engage in this process of inner work in order to achieve spiritual progress, which enables them to more completely embody their best potential. The process of personal development is a journey that is not only difficult but also rewarding. It is characterized by periods of struggle and breakthrough, and it ultimately results in increased satisfaction, joy, and freedom.

When it comes to further exploration, the engagement with the community and the sharing of experiences are both extremely important factors. The journey is made more meaningful by the direction, encouragement, and company that is provided along the road by fellow searchers, mentors, and teachers who provide their knowledge and support while traveling. Communities, whether they are formed in physical venues or through digital platforms, provide individuals with a sense of belonging and a shared purpose, which serves to remind them that they are not alone in their pursuit of understanding and development.

Exploration of the holy and the mystical is a route that leads to a more profound connection, not just with oneself but also with the divine, the earth, and all other beings. A recognition of the sacredness of life and the interrelated web of existence is suggested as a result of this possibility. Individuals can create a profound sense of reverence and thankfulness for the marvel of existence by engaging in practices such as prayer, ritual, and contact with nature. This will help them develop a harmonious relationship with the environment that surrounds them.

An invitation to participate in service is also a call to encourage further exploration. As people become more aware of their connectivity and the potential that lies within them, they are naturally drawn to make contributions that contribute to the well-being of others and the planet. Exploration is not merely a voyage for the purpose of gaining personal benefit; rather, it is a road that leads to increased compassion and empathy, as well as a desire to have a beneficial impact on the world. The insights that are learned on the spiritual path are turned into meaningful action in the world through the practice of acts of kindness, advocacy for justice, and the stewardship of the land.

In conclusion, the offer to start on a voyage of boundless discovery is an invitation included inside the encouragement for further study. It is an invitation to delve more deeply into the mysteries of existence, to embrace the unknown with bravery and curiosity, and to make a commitment to a path that will lead to personal and collective transformation. Individuals have the opportunity to discover fundamental truths, experience tremendous healing and connection, and contribute to the building of a world that is more mindful and compassionate through the course of this journey. There are countless opportunities for personal development, comprehension, and the discovery of one's actual nature and purpose that can be found along the path of exploration, which is accessible to anybody who seeks it with an adventurous spirit.

Final Thoughts on Sex Magic as a Path to Self-Discovery and Connection

There is a one-of-a-kind way to find oneself and make connections through the practice of sex magic, which is a technique that combines the powerful forces of sexuality with spirituality. It encourages people to go into the innermost parts of themselves, utilizing sexual energy not only for the purpose of pleasure or reproduction, but also as a potent instrument for transformation, manifestation, and profound communion with oneself, other people, and the universe. Reflecting on sex magic as a complex journey, this section highlights the relevance of sex magic, the challenges that it presents, and the transforming potential that it offers for those who embark upon its path.

In its most fundamental form, sex magic is an assertion of the sacredness of sexuality, which is a concept that is frequently ignored in contemporary debate on sexual sexuality. The act of lovemaking and sexual expression is elevated to the level of a spiritual discipline through the practice of sex magic, which redefines sexuality as a supernatural and powerful force. Individuals are encouraged to approach their sexuality with reverence, mindfulness, and intention as a result of this recontextualization, which results in the development of a deeper appreciation for their bodies, desires, and the exchange of energy that takes place during sexual experiences.

The path of sex magic is one of self-discovery, and it encourages practitioners to explore the unexplored frontiers of their wants, fears, and potential that has not yet been realized. An individual is urged to confront and integrate aspects of their shadow self through the intentional use of sexual energy, which in turn facilitates a process of healing and wholeness for the individual. Taking this trip inward reveals the interdependence of one's sexual, emotional, and spiritual dimensions, providing insights into the ways in which these forces form one's reality and experiences.

In addition, sex magic acts as a bridge to connection, whether it is connection to oneself, connection to one's partner, or connection to the broader pattern of existence. During solitary practices, sex magic helps to cultivate a more profound connection with oneself, which in turn boosts feelings of self-love and confidence, as well as the capacity to bring one's wishes into physical form. Bonds can be strengthened, closeness can be deepened, and a shared spiritual experience that transcends the physical sphere can be created through the use of this technique in paired practices. Beyond the realms of the personal and interpersonal, sex magic makes it possible to establish a link to the universal life force. This enables practitioners to tap into the collective energy that permeates everything, which in turn enhances their sense of togetherness and belonging.

The incorporation of sex magic into everyday life and interpersonal relationships, on the other hand, is not without its difficulties. In order to accomplish this, it is necessary to overcome personal limitations and vulnerabilities, as well as to navigate the taboos and misconceptions that are prevalent in society regarding sexuality and magic. The technique necessitates a high level of honesty, communication, and ethical deliberation, particularly with regard to ensuring that all actions are conducted with consent and with respect for limits. Furthermore, in order to avoid imbalance or misalignment with one's aims, it is necessary to engage in continuous self-reflection, self-care, and mindfulness in order to stay in a state of balance and harmony when it comes to the utilization of sexual energy.

The potential for sex magic to bring about transformation is enormous, despite the difficulties that it presents. It provides a means of achieving personal empowerment by enabling individuals to harness their sexual energy for the purposes of healing, creativity, and the actualization of their most profound dreams. The practice has the potential to bring about deep spiritual experiences, which might include gaining insights into the interconnectedness of all life and coming to terms with one's own divine nature. Individuals have the potential to experience a tremendous sense of aliveness, joy, and fulfillment through the practice of sex magic. This transformation is founded on the genuine expression of their sexuality and spirituality.

In conclusion, sex magic is a potent and holy process that leads to the discovery of oneself and the establishment of connections. By doing so, it encourages individuals to go into the innermost parts of their being, to rethink their conception of sexuality, and to harness this powerful force for the purpose of fostering personal and spiritual development. Practitioners of sex magic can unlock new aspects of their life by approaching it with intention, reverence, and an open heart. This allows them to cultivate a deeper connection to themselves, others, and the cosmos. Sex magic is a journey of transformation and empowerment that provides a one-of-a-kind opportunity to engage with the wonders of life. It encourages individuals to embrace the whole spectrum of human experience with bravery, curiosity, and love.

CONCLUSION

As we come to the end of our journey through "Passion Potions and Love Rituals: A Beginner's Guide to Sex Magic," it is fitting to pause and reflect on the profound insights and transformative experiences that have unfolded along the way. From the ancient mysteries of sexual energy to the practical rituals and techniques of modern sex magic, we have explored the depths of human desire and the heights of spiritual ecstasy, discovering a path of profound connection, healing, and empowerment.

Throughout this book, we have traversed the vast landscape of sex magic, delving into its history, principles, and practices with curiosity, reverence, and a spirit of open inquiry. We have learned that sex magic is not merely a collection of esoteric rituals or arcane knowledge but a living, breathing tradition that speaks to the deepest longings of the human soul—a longing for connection, for meaning, and for the realization of our fullest potential as spiritual beings.

At the heart of sex magic lies the recognition that sexuality is a sacred and potent force, capable of catalyzing profound transformation and awakening. By harnessing the power of sexual energy—through intention, visualization, and conscious practice—we can unlock the hidden potentials of our bodies, minds, and spirits, tapping into the vast reservoir of creative energy that animates the universe itself.

But sex magic is more than just a means to an end; it is a journey of self-discovery, a path of self-realization that invites us to explore the depths of our own desires, fears, and aspirations. Through the practices of sex magic, we confront our limitations, our insecurities, and our illusions, and we learn to embrace the fullness of our being with love, compassion, and acceptance.

In the pages of this book, we have encountered a myriad of tools and techniques for harnessing the transformative power of sex magic—from visualization exercises and breathing techniques to the creation of love elixirs and the invocation of sacred deities. Yet, amidst the diversity of practices and rituals, a common thread runs through them all: the recognition that love is the ultimate force that binds us together, that connects us to ourselves, to each other, and to the divine.

Throughout our exploration of sex magic, we have emphasized the importance of ethical conduct, consent, and mutual respect, recognizing that the power of sex magic carries with it a great responsibility—a responsibility to ourselves, to our partners, and to the world around us. By approaching sex magic with integrity, humility, and reverence, we honor the sacredness of the practice and create space for profound healing, growth, and transformation.

As we bring our journey to a close, let us carry with us the lessons and insights that we have gleaned along the way. Let us remember that sex magic is not a destination but a journey—a journey of self-discovery, self-expression, and self-transcendence. Let us continue to explore the depths of our desires, the heights of our aspirations, and the mysteries of our own hearts with courage, curiosity, and compassion.

And above all, let us remember that the true magic of sex lies not in the attainment of our desires or the fulfillment of our fantasies but in the recognition of our own inherent worthiness, our own inherent beauty, and our own inherent divinity. For in the embrace of love—in all its forms and manifestations—we find the true source of our power, joy, and fulfillment.

So, dear reader, as you close the pages of this book and embark on your own journey of sex magic, may you carry with you the wisdom of the ages, the fire of passion, and the light of love. May you embrace the fullness of your being with courage and grace, and may you shine brightly as a beacon of love, healing, and transformation in the world.

In the end, it is not the rituals or techniques that define us but the love that we bring to them, the love that we share with ourselves, each other, and the universe. And in that love, we find the true magic of sex—the magic of connection, of healing, and of transcendence.

Thank you for joining me on this journey. May your path be blessed with love, joy, and infinite possibilities.

Thank you for buying and reading/ listening to our book. If you found this book useful/ helpful please take a few minutes and leave a review on the platform where you purchased our book. Your feedback matters greatly to us.